MW01062477

THE GREAT
BOOK OF COLORADO

The Crazy History of Colorado with Amazing Random Facts & Trivia

A Trivia Nerds Guide
to the History of the
United States Vol.11

BILL O'NEILL

DON'T FORGET YOUR
FREE BOOKS

GET THEM FOR FREE ON
WWW.TRIVIABILL.COM

CONTENTS

CHAPTER TWO
COLORADO'S POP CULTURE 34

CHAPTER THREE
COLORADO'S INVENTIONS, IDEAS, AND MORE...58

CHAPTER FIVE
COLORADO'S SPORTS 111

INTRODUCTION

How much do you know about the state of Colorado?

Of course you know it's one of the top places in the country to go skiing and that it's very nature lover's dream, but how much do you really know about that state? Do you know how Colorado got its name or how it earned the nickname of the "Centennial State"? Do you know what led people to migrate to the state or why its population continues to increase to this day?

Did you know that dinosaurs once roamed Colorado? Do you know which dinosaurs were named after fossils that were found in the state?

Do you know which products, inventions, and fast food chains came out of the state of Colorado? Do you know which popular candy was started in Colorado? Do you know about the sweet ice cream treat that was invented in Cripple Creek? Do you know about the famous Coloradan sandwich that Elvis Presley once traveled across the country for?

Do you know which hotel inspired a popular Stephen King novel? Do you know which celebrities hail from the state? How much do you know about Colorado's sports teams? Do you know which major sporting event the state decided not to host?

If you have ever wondered any of these things about the Centennial State, then you've come to the right place! This isn't your average book about Colorado. Here, you'll read fun and interesting stories about the state. Whether you live in the Centennial State or you're planning a trip, you're bound to learn something about Colorado that you don't already know.

Colorado is a state that's rich in history and culture. We will bounce around as we look at some of the most interesting historical facts about the Centennial State. You will learn more about Colorado's pop culture, inventions, attractions, sports, and so much more!

This book is broken up into six easy to follow chapters that will help you learn everything you need to know about the state of Colorado. At the end of each chapter, you'll find a Q&A so you can test your knowledge on what you've just read.

Some of the facts you will learn about in this book are shocking. Some of them are sad, while some of them are eerie. But the one thing that all of these facts have in common is that they're *all* interesting!

Once you have finished reading this book, you'll walk away with a wealth of knowledge. You'll even impress your history teacher!

This book will answer the following questions:

How did Colorado get its name?

Why is it nicknamed the "Centennial State"?

Which patriotic song was written in the state?

Which famous comic strip characters were based on actual people from Colorado?

Which historical sporting event was first held in the Centennial State?

Are there really living dinosaurs still roaming the earth in Colorado?

What are some of the most haunted spots in the state?

And so much more!

CHAPTER ONE

COLORADO'S HISTORY AND OTHER FACTS

Sure, you know Colorado is located in the Rocky Mountain region of the Western U.S. and that it's a top skiing location, but how much else do you really know about the state? Do you know how Colorado got its name or what it means? Do you have any idea why it was given the nickname the "Centennial State"? Do you know which patriotic song was written in the state or what prehistoric creatures once roamed the state? Do you know what has led people to migrate to the state? Do you know why Colorado's population continues to increase to this day? Read on to find out the answers to these and other questions.

How Colorado Got Its Name

Have you ever wondered where Colorado got its name? The word "Colorado" comes from the Spanish language, but do you know what it means or why the state was named this?

During the late 1500s, early Spanish explorers in the area named a river after the reddish color of the silt that it carried from the mountains. The name they gave it was Rio Colorado. *Rio* means "river" and *Colorado* means "colored red," so the translation is "red river." The Rio Colorado is the river that we know of, today, as the Colorado River.

There are a couple of theories on how the state got its name, but no one really knows for sure. Some say that the then-territory of Colorado was named after the Colorado River. It has also been said that the state may have been named after Colorado City (or today's Colorado Springs).

Regardless of where, exactly, the state got its name from, it can be agreed that its name meaning is "colored red." And it's a fitting name when you consider the red sandstone and clay that can be found throughout the state.

Why It's Known as the "Centennial State"

By now you already know that Colorado is nicknamed the "Centennial State." Do you know how the state earned this nickname?

First, it's important to note that Colorado had an incredibly long path to statehood. The territory was first acquired by the United States in 1803 as a part of the Louisiana Purchase. Once the then-territory was ready to become a state, it wasn't an easy or quick process. In fact, it took a total of *16 years* for it to finally become a state.

When the territory of Colorado first attempted to join the Union, it was vetoed by President Andrew Johnson due to his own political agenda. It was actually the next president, Ulysses S. Grant, who accepted the admittance and granted Colorado its statehood.

Colorado became the 38th state to join the union on August 1,1876, but the celebration allegedly began on the 4th of July—exactly 100 years after the Declaration of Independence was signed. This is where the state got its official nickname the "Centennial State" from!

This Patriotic Song Was Written in the State

Did you know one of the United States' most patriotic songs was written in Colorado? Do you know which one? One hint: it's *not* "The Star-Spangled Banner."

The lyrics of the song "America the Beautiful" were written while Katherine Lee Bates was at the top of Pikes Peak, which overlooks Colorado Springs, back in 1893, according to the writer herself. What you might not know is that the words weren't originally intended to be a song. The song lyrics were first published as a poem that was called "America." It first made its debut in the 4th of July edition of the church periodical, *The Congregationalist*, in 1895.

It wasn't until 1910 that Bates' poem became a song. It was paired with the tune "Materna," which was composed by Samuel Ward in 1882.

How Denver Got Its Name and Nickname

Have you ever wondered where Denver got its name? With many places in Colorado having Spanish names, Denver might seem a little out of place. That's because Denver was named after someone.

Denver City was named after James W. Denver, who was governor of the Kansas Territory. The name Denver City was given by General William Larimer in 1858. Larimer hoped that the name of the town would win favor with Governor Denver in an attempt at making it the county seat of Arapahoe County. Larimer didn't realize that Governor Denver already had plans to resign.

Larimer's wish came true anyway, though. After the Colorado Territory was created in 1861, Denver City was incorporated as the Arapahoe County seat. In 1867, Denver City became the territory's capital and, later, the permanent state capital in 1881 after a statewide ballot. At this time, the city's name was shortened to Denver.

You probably know by now that Denver is nicknamed

the "Mile High City". This is because Denver is—you guessed it—exactly one mile high!

In fact, the 13th step of the State Capitol building is at 5,280 feet (or exactly one mile) above sea level.

Denver's altitude has a bigger effect on the city than you might think. For starters, golf balls travel 10% farther than they do at sea level.

A surprising effect of Denver's altitude is that alcoholic drinks are more likely to get you drunk than when you drink at sea level.

The sun also feels warmer, thanks to the thinner atmosphere.

Your coffee will also be colder than it would be at sea level, however. This is because water boils at 202 degrees Fahrenheit (or 94 degrees Celsius) in Denver vs. 212 degrees Fahrenheit (100 degrees Celsius) in other places.

Denver is not an ideal location to own a bagel shop. It has been said that bagels tend to come out tasting like dog biscuits when boiled.

The effects of Denver's high altitude aren't always good ones, unfortunately. High altitudes have also been linked to health problems. You're more likely to experience breathing problems, sleep difficulties, feet swelling, dizziness, light-headedness, and nausea. These symptoms of altitude sickness are the result of decreased oxygen.

People Were Drawn to Colorado Due to the Pikes Peak Gold Rush

Did you know that Colorado was part of the Wild West? Many early pioneers first migrated to the state in hopes of striking it big time with gold. In fact, the Colorado Gold Rush was what drew most people to the state in the first place.

It wasn't until the 1850s that gold was found in Colorado. But once it did, pioneers embarked on a journey to the west in search of gold. This is what sparked the Colorado Gold Rush, which was also known as the "Pikes Peak Gold Rush." (The gold rush was named after Pikes Peak, which is one of Colorado's 53 mountain peaks known as "fourteeners," which have an elevation of more than 14,000 feet).

The Pikes Peak Gold Rush led to a huge population boom. In fact, a lot of Colorado's current cities were founded during the Pikes Peak Gold Rush. These include Denver, Boulder, Central City, Black Hawk, and Breckenridge. There was also Cripple Creek, where one of the biggest gold strikes in history happened.

Just how much did the Pikes Peak Gold Rush impact Colorado's population? To put things into perspective, there were no people living in today's Denver metropolitan area during 1858. Within 30 years, however, Colorado was home to nearly 200,000 people.

Although the Colorado Gold Rush is often still referred to as the "Pikes Peak Gold Rush," the truth is that gold mining near the mountain didn't take place until the 1890s—*long* after the Gold Rush had already earned this nickname.

So, where did the infamous Pikes Peak Gold Rush nickname come from if gold wasn't being mined near the mountain when the name came about?

The view of Pikes Peak on the western horizon was a symbol of hope for people migrating to Colorado. The image of the mountain represented the Gold Rush in the Rocky Mountains.

The nickname turned out to be an appropriate one, however. During the 1890s, the Cripple Creek strike happened, which drew people near the mountain in droves. The strike happened at Stratton's Independence Mine and Mill, where an estimated 200,000 ounces—or 6,200 kg—of gold was found between the years of 1893 and 1899.

There Have Also Been Two Other Colorado Population Booms

Did you know that Colorado's population can also be attributed to an illness? Although the Pikes Peak Gold Rush is what first drew a lot of people to

Colorado, there was something else that led people to migrate to the state—something much darker. That would be tuberculosis and the hope for a cure.

During the 1800s, tuberculosis—or TB—was the No. 1 cause of death in America. Physicians during that time felt that fresh air, sunshine, and high altitudes would help cure the disease, making Colorado a prime place for TB sufferers to live. It earned the nickname of the "World's Sanitorium."

During the 1860s, people infected with TB started migrating to the then-territory in hopes of benefiting from it. In the early 1860s, facilities for TB patients began to open in Denver, Colorado Springs, and Boulder. The facilities were like health spa resorts where patients would go to relax, take in the fresh air, and sometimes drink mineral water. Many hospitals opened in the form of Sanitoriums to treat TB. More often than not, patients would die at these facilities or hospitals.

Many tuberculosis sufferers bought one-way tickets to Colorado in hopes of being cured of their illness. When they arrived, however, they realized they were unable to afford to stay at one of the TB facilities. Some "facilities" started being held at camps with tents. This, in turn, created a homeless population in the state.

There were even some famous people who came to Colorado in hopes of seeking TB treatment for themselves or their family. Some of these included a young Robert Frost, Golda Meer, Robert Speer, and Doc Holladay (who died in Glenwood Springs).

People continued to flock to Colorado in hopes of seeking the cure until the early 1900s. During the 1940s, antibiotic treatment for TB was discovered and no one needed to travel to Colorado anymore in hopes of curing the disease.

The Pikes Peak Gold Rush and the Tuberculosis Boom are what first paved the way to Colorado's population. But did you know that there's another Colorado population boom that's currently ongoing?

Ever since Colorado became one of the first states to legalize recreational marijuana in 2012, there has been a huge influx of people moving to the state.

In fact, so many people have moved to the state as a result of the "Cannabis Boom" that it's had detrimental effects on Colorado's housing market. There was an affordable housing crisis, with home prices skyrocketing and making it nearly impossible for anyone to afford to live in Denver except for the wealthy.

Even in spite of the three population booms that brought people to Colorado, the Centennial State still has a very low population.

Colorado's population was approximately 5.6 million in 2018, which was a 13.25% increase from 2010. For comparison's sake, New York City's population is about 8.2 million and Los Angeles' population is approximately 3.8 million.

Colorado only ranks at No. 21 in terms of most populated U.S. states.

Denver is a Huge City for Craft Beer

Denver has a long history of beer, dating back to when the city was first founded in 1859. When the early pioneers and miners migrated to the city in search of gold, barrooms and saloons began to open throughout the city's downtown. In fact, it has even been said that the first permanent structure in Denver was a saloon! The first city government was even formed in a saloon called the Apollo Hall.

One of Denver City's earliest laws banned people from selling liquor on the streets, as well as from wagons or tents.

Today, Denver is still a huge city when it comes to craft beer.

It might surprise you to learn that Denver ranks at No. 2 for cities in the U.S. with the most breweries. With more than 158 breweries, Denver is only surpassed by Chicago, the Beer Capital of America.

There are 15 craft breweries for every 500,000 people in the state. This means that Colorado is No. 5 in terms of states with the most craft breweries.

Denver's most popular breweries are Great Divide Brewing Company and Wynkoop Brewing Company.

And that's not all. Colorado, as a whole, is a huge state for breweries. In fact, four of the top 50 breweries in America are located in the Centennial State. These include:

- New Belgium Brewing, Co. (Fort Collins, Colorado)
- CANarchy (Longmont, Colorado)
- Odell Brewing, Co. (Fort Collins, Colorado)
- Left Hand Brewing Company (Longmont, Colorado)

New Belgium Brewing is also the first wind-powered brewery in America and the largest of its kind in the entire world.

Denver is also famous for the Great American Beer Festival, which is held every autumn in the Mile High City. According to the *Guinness Book of World Records*, there's no other place in the world where you can find more beers on tap than at the festival. The three-day festival, which is held at the Colorado Convention Center, offers 3,000 beer samples from over 600 breweries from all around the country. The beers are arranged geographically. The festival draws in approximately 50,000 beer lovers each year.

Denver also hosts Denver Beer Fest every year.

This Dental Discovery Was Made in Colorado Springs

Did you know that fluoride was first discovered in Colorado Springs during the 1900s?

Back in 1901, a young dentist named Frederick McKay opened a practice in Colorado Springs. He couldn't believe what he found there. His patients from Colorado Springs had brown stains on their teeth, sometimes with the entire tooth being covered in splotches the color of chocolate.

Dr. McKay didn't understand what was causing this mystery dental disorder among his patients and began looking for an answer. He couldn't find any dental literature during the time that mentioned the brown stains his patients were experiencing.

Colorado Springs residents had their own theories. Some believed that it was from eating too much pork, while others thought they were consuming bad milk. Still, others thought it was due to drinking calcium-rich water.

Other dentists in the area weren't interested in solving the problem. But Dr. McKay made headway with local practitioners in the area, who wanted to get to the bottom of the cause of "Colorado Brown Stain."

In 1909, a dental researcher named Dr. G.V. Black came to Colorado Springs to collaborate with Dr.

McKay on the problem. Black originally didn't think that such a phenomenon was possible without making its way into dental literature, but his interest was piqued after a study found that nine out of 10 children born in Colorado Springs had the brown stains.

Dr. G.V. Black studied fluorosis for six years until he died in 1915. While he was alive, he and Dr. McKay made two major discoveries:

1). The brown spots—which they referred to as "mottled enamel"—were caused by developmental imperfections. This meant that Colorado Springs residents whose teeth had already calcified without being affected by the stains didn't have their teeth turn later.

2). The teeth that *were* affected by Colorado Brown Stain were resistant to tooth decay.

Dr. McKay had a theory that there was an ingredient in the Colorado Springs water that caused this enamel problem—and his theory turned out to be right. After 30 years of research and analyzing water supplies in other states where people were experiencing the same problem, it was discovered that there was fluoride in the water of those affected. The condition eventually came to be known as fluorosis.

McKay's findings paved the way to fluoride being

used to help prevent tooth decay—and it all started out in Colorado Springs.

Colorado is the Only Place in the U.S. Where You Can Stand in Four States at Once

Have you ever wanted to stand in four places at once? Did you know that you can do just that in Colorado? In fact, southwest Colorado is the only spot in the entire United States where the corners of four states meet!

Colorado's southwest corner borders the states of Utah, New Mexico, and Arizona.

The Four Corners Monument is the legal divider of where the four states intersect. It's the only spot in America where you can stand in four states at the same time. It's located at approximately 37° north latitude with 109° 03' west longitude.

Located on the Colorado Plateau west of Highway 160, the monument marks more than just where the four states meet. It also marks the boundaries of two Native American tribal government: the Navajo Nation and the Ute Mountain Ute Tribe Reservation.

The monument is maintained by the Navajo Nation Parks and Recreation Department. In fact, when you visit the monument, you will find that the flags of the Navajo Nation and Ute Nation fly alongside the flags of Colorado, New Mexico, Arizona, and Utah.

It is a tradition for people to take pictures at that monument. Although many people post their pictures to Instagram and other social media platforms today, the tradition of taking photos at the monument has been going on since the early 1900s when people would travel from far distances just to take a photo at the monument. Many people sit or stand on the disk with their friends, while others take photos kissing over the monument. What this means is that you can expect a long line when you visit the monument.

Today, Four Corners Monument is a huge tourist attraction, drawing in thousands of people each year who can knock standing in four states at once off their bucket list.

Colorado is Home to a Large Population of This Animal

Did you know that Colorado is home to North America's largest population of elk? It wasn't always that way, however.

It might surprise you to learn that elk play a key role in Colorado's history. Elk, which were named *wapiti* by the Shawnee Indians, migrated across the Bering Strait from Asia more than 100,000 years ago. They then roamed for Canada and into Mexico, arriving in Colorado approximately 8,000 to 10,000 years ago.

Elk became an important source of food for Colorado's indigenous people, including the Ute, Navajo, Apache, Hopi, Zuni, and Havasupai. They also hunted the elk for clothing and tools.

As white settlers moved to the west during the Colorado Gold Rush, populations of elk began to diminish. It wasn't until the early 1900s that Colorado implemented hunting regulations in an effort to conserve the elk that remained in the state. The U.S. Forest Service found that approximately 500 to 1,000 elk were residing in the state during 1910. Between 1903 and 1933, elk hunting was banned completely. By the 1930s, elk populations had begun to rebound.

Today, it's estimated that approximately 280,000 elk live in Colorado, making it the largest population in North America. These elk are spread out across millions of acres of both publicly and privately-owned land.

Tourists come from miles around in hopes of seeing the elk. Meanwhile, Colorado has become a prime state for elk hunting, which is encouraged these days to prevent overgrazing. It's been estimated that 250,000 hunters visit Colorado each year, generally hunting about 50,000 elk. Culling—in which fertile females are killed off—is also common in the state to help prevent overpopulation.

This Unique Gemstone Was Found in the State

Did you know one of the largest diamonds to ever be found in North America was found in Colorado?

The diamond was the 5th largest found in not only the United States but in all of North America. Earning the name of the "Colorado Diamond," the gemstone was found at the Kelsey Lake mine in 1996.

It was a 28.3-carat yellow diamond. The gemstone was cut and polished by the infamous New York diamond cutter Bill Goldberg, who yielded a 5.39-carat stone from it. The Colorado Diamond was sold for $87,500.

Colorado is Home to A Lot of Ghost Towns

Did you know that Colorado is home to *a lot* of ghost towns? In fact, the state has nearly as many dead towns as it has active ones.

The high number of ghost towns is a result of the mining industry. Colorado was a state that had a mining boom. The state was known for its silver industry, in particular. Then in 1893, silver was devalued and many of the mining towns were abandoned. Mill towns that serviced the mining towns were also affected.

Today, there are approximately 500 ghost towns and 650 active towns in Colorado.

Some of the most well-known Coloradan ghost towns, which are top tourist attractions, include:

- **St. Elmo** – Recognized as one of Colorado's most well-preserved ghost towns, you can expect to find wooden storefronts and a dusty main street.
- **Ashcroft** – Located near Aspen, CO., you can take a tour of this ghost town. The jail, saloons, and an old stable have all been preserved.
- **Teller City** – This former silver mining camp was booming during the early 1880s. Today, you can see the remains of log cabins, saloons, and the beauty of the forested area.
- **Tomboy** – Perhaps the most unique aspect of this ghost town is the "Social Tunnel," which is where women met up with Tomboy mine men in the area for some fun times.
- **Dearfield** – Today, three buildings still stand in this old ghost town, which was once the only all-black settlement in Colorado. Once home to more than 700 African-Americans, the town died during the Great Depression and Dust Bowl era.

Some of the other most well-known ghost towns in Colorado include Capitol City, Ohio City, Alta, Nevadaville, Mayflower Gulch, Independence, Vicksburg, Winfield, Goldfield, and Animas Forks.

Two of the Most Tragic Mass Shootings in History Happened in Colorado

Back in April of 1999, the Columbine High School massacre took place at Columbine High School in Littleton, Colorado when two teenage boys went on a shooting spree before taking their own lives. The massacre resulted in 13 fatalities and 20 wounded victims. Although it was not the deadliest school shooting to ever occur in the U.S., it *was* the worst at the time it occurred.

Tragically, the shooting has also been the inspiration of other school shootings throughout American history.

The Columbine High School massacre wasn't the only famous shooting to ever take place in the state.

In 2012, James Holmes shot and killed 12 people and injured another 70 people at a movie theater in Aurora, Colorado. Holmes is currently serving 12 consecutive life sentences, along with 3,318 years without parole, for the massacre.

Both of these shootings were significant to American history, sparking the debate about gun control throughout the U.S.

This City in Colorado Was Once Nicknamed the "Sex Change Capital of the World"

Did you know that Colorado was once home to the "Sex Change Capital of the World"? This nickname was given to Trinidad, Colorado where a large number of transgender operations have taken place.

The majority of sex change operations between the years of 1969 and 2003 took place in Trinidad. In fact, it has been estimated that approximately 65% of the world's sex change surgeries were performed in Trinidad by Dr. Stanley Biber.

Dr. Biber's first sex change operation took place in 1969 after a local social worker asked if he could perform the surgery for her. Biber used diagrams and also consulted with a New York surgeon before performing the procedure.

There weren't many doctors who performed the surgery at the time, and Biber was recognized as a good surgeon. It was estimated that at one point, he was performing approximately four sex-change surgeries on a daily basis.

Many people who underwent his procedure began to say they were "taking a trip to Trinidad," due to the town name.

In 2003, a transgender surgeon named Dr. Marci Bowers took over Dr. Biber's practice. Dr. Bowers relocated, moving the practice to San Mateo, California.

A documentary about Dr. Bowers and the practice called *Trinidad* was released in 2008.

Colorado Was Once a Hotspot for Dinosaurs

Did you know that one of the largest preserved sets of dinosaur tracks on the entire planet can be found in Colorado? The tracks, which are located in the Picketwire Canyon in the Comanche National Grasslands, are the largest in North America!

During the Jurassic Period, more than 150 million years ago, the climate in Southeast Colorado was tropical. The Purgatoire River was part of a shallow lake where dinosaurs, including the Apatosaurus and the Allosaurus, wandered and left behind their footprints—1,900 footprints, to be exact. The footprints make up more than 130 trackways, which can be found in the bedrock along the Purgatoire River banks.

And that's not all! A number of really cool dinosaur fossils were discovered throughout the state, some of which even earned these dinosaurs their names.

In 1874, the first ever T. Rex fossil was discovered near Golden, Colorado. This fossil didn't gain a lot of fame, however, with many T. Rex fossils discovered across the U.S. gaining more popularity. This is because the fossil wasn't the first full T. Rex fossil to ever be discovered. It was only the T. Rex's teeth.

The most remarkable and famous dinosaur fossil find in Colorado's history is that of the Stegosaurus. The first Stegosaurus fossil to *ever* be discovered in the entire world was found in Morrison, Colorado back in 1876. For this reason, it might not surprise you to learn that Colorado's official state fossil and their official state dinosaur is the Stegosaurus.

The fossil was also what gave the dinosaur its name. Paleontologist Othneil C. Marsh named the fossil and, essentially, the dinosaur that it was derived from, the "Stegosaurus." The name means "roofed lizard" or "covered lizard."

Marsh also named two other dinosaurs based on fossils that were discovered in the Centennial State, including the Allosaurus, the deadliest meat-eating dinosaur of the late Jurassic period. The word "Allosaurus" means "different lizard." The first Allosaurus fossil to ever be discovered was found in Morrison's Formation in 1869.

The third dinosaur named by Othneil C. Marsh is the Ornithomimus (which means "bird mimic"), which was also first uncovered in Colorado. The fossil that earned the dinosaur its name was found in the Denver Formation in 1889. The ostrich-like theropod was thought to be able to gallop faster than 30 miles per hour, making it a prehistoric Road Runner.

The first Torvosaurus, which is closely linked to the Allosaurus, was discovered near Delta, CO in 1971.

Colorado's history as a fossils state has been well-preserved with numerous dinosaur attractions throughout the state. You can see a number of different dinosaur fossils at Dinosaur Ridge, an outdoor museum in Morrison, Colorado. You can even hike in the Stegosaurus's footsteps.

RANDOM FACTS

1. Colorado has not been the birthplace of any U.S. President or Vice President to date. It is one of 29 states that has never birthed a president.

2. Colorado is the 8th largest state in America in terms of land mass. It has the highest elevation of any U.S. state, with an average altitude of 6,800 feet and peaks that reach more than 14,000 feet. Approximately 75% of the United States' land over 10,000 feet can also be found in Colorado. Colorado is also the highest state in the country. It's entirely above 1,000 meters' elevation.

3. There's a lot of debate among Colorado natives on what they should be referred to. While "Coloradans" is most commonly used when describing people from Colorado, others refer to them as "Coloradoans." Then there are still some who prefer the more political term "Coloradicals."

4. Denver is home to the famous Colfax Avenue, the longest continuous street in America. Colfax Ave is a commercial street that serves as the main street, running from east to west in the Denver metro area. The street is 49.5 miles long, spanning from Lakewood, CO to Aurora, CO. Legend has it that *Playboy* magazine once called

it "the longest, wickedest street in America", though there's no proof that this ever actually happened.

5. It's sunny approximately 300 days in Colorado each year. This makes it one of the sunniest places in the entire U.S. It's also possible to go skiing *and* swimming on the same day due to the differences in temperatures at varying elevations found throughout the state.

6. The Royal Gorge Bridge, which is near Canon City, is the highest suspension bridge in the entire world. The bridge, which spans the Arkansas River, has a height of 1,053 feet. The bridge is three feet taller than the Empire State Building.

7. The largest flat-top mountain in the world is Grand Mesa, which is located in Western Colorado. With an elevation of 11, 332 feet and a width of 40 miles, the mountain is named after it's flat "Mesa" (which means "table" in Spanish). The Mesa Scenic Byway is a great way to experience the mountain's beauty. The Grand Mesa is a popular hiking spot during the summer months and a popular skiing and snowshoeing spot in the winter.

8. The highest auto tunnel in the world is located in Colorado! With an elevation of 11,000 feet, the

Dwight Eisenhower Memorial Tunnel sees an average of more than 26,000 vehicles a day.

9. The first license plate in the United States was issued in Denver, Colorado back in 1908.

10. Colorado is one of the only states in America where skijoring can be found. Never heard of it before? It's a sport in which a horse pulls a skier who's holding onto a rope over snow jumps and through obstacles. Skijoring takes place in Leadville, Colorado every March.

11. Colorado Springs is home to the United States Air Force Academy. The Air Force Academy's Cadet Chapel sees over 500,000 visitors each year.

12. Colorado is home to some unique towns. Dove Creek, Colorado claims the title of the "Pinto Bean Capital of the World"! Loveland, Colorado is known as the "Sweetheart City." Meanwhile, Rocky Ford, CO has gained the nickname of the "Sweet Melon Capital of the World."

13. The town of Fruita, Colorado celebrates "Mike the Headless Chicken Day." The day is celebrated in honor of an unusual event that took place in the town many years ago. Back in 1945, a farmer by the name of L.A. Olsen cut off his chicken's head. Olsen had planned to have the bird for dinner. However, the chicken, whose

name was Mike, ended up living for another four years without a head.

14. Like every state, Colorado is home to a number of strange laws. It's illegal to ride a horse while you're under the influence, show a car at a dealership on a Sunday or mutilate a rock in a Colorado state park. In Denver, it's illegal to lend your vacuum to your neighbor. In Logan County, it's illegal for a man to kiss a woman while she's sleeping. Perhaps the strangest is a law that says dandelions may not be grown within the city limits of Pueblo, Colorado.

15. The Lower Downtown area of Denver is commonly referred to as the LoDo. LoDo is Denver's oldest neighborhood.

16. Denver has the largest city park system in all of America. The city is home to 205 parks within city limits, as well as 20,000 acres of parks in the surrounding mountains.

17. Grizzly bears used to be frequently sighted in Colorado. However, it's been decades since they have been seen. The last reported grizzly bear in the state was in 1979 when Ed Wiseman was hunting near the Continental Divide. The bear attacked Wiseman after the hunter had accidentally cornered him. Wiseman fought back, however. He used a handheld arrow to stab the

bear until it died. No one believed Wiseman's story at first, but he was given a lie detector test and passed.

18. Colorado's official state motto is "Nil Sin Numine." In Latin, this translates to "Nothing without Providence."

19. Colorado is home to the highest ski lift in all of North America. The Imperial Express Superchair at Breckenridge Ski Resort drops skiers off at nearly 13,000 feet.

20. The United States Penitentiary, Administrative Maximum Facility, also known as USP Florence ADMAX, is located in Fremont County, Colorado. The SuperMax prison is the highest security prison in the U.S. and has earned the nickname of "Alcatraz in the Rockies." Most of the inmates are terrorists, organized crime figures, or double agents. One of the most notable inmates is Dzhokhar Tsarnaev, a participant of the Boston Marathon bombing.

Test Yourself – Questions

1. The meaning of the word "Colorado" is:

   a. Colored red
   b. Red mountains
   c. Red river

2. The largest flat-top mountain in the world is:

   a. Pikes Peak
   b. Rocky Mountain
   c. Grand Mesa

3. The first Stegosaurus fossil was found in Colorado in what year?

   a. 1976
   b. 1876
   c. 1926

4. Denver is home to the largest:

   a. City park system in America
   b. Park fountain in North America
   c. Park in the world

5. The first ___ in the United States was issued in Denver, CO.

   a. Pilot's license
   b. Nursing license
   c. Driver's license

Answers

1. a.
2. c.
3. b.
4. a.
5. c.

CHAPTER TWO

COLORADO'S POP CULTURE

How much do you know about Colorado's pop culture? Do you know which famous TV dad is from the state? Do you know which Colorado haunted hotel was the inspiration behind a famous novel to movie adaptation? Do you know which *Gilmore Girls* actress hails from the Centennial State? Do you know which famous comic strip characters originated from the state? Read on to find out the answers to these questions and learn more about Colorado's pop culture!

The Movie That Brought This Former Celebrity Couple Together Was Filmed in Colorado

While they might no longer be a couple, Brad Pitt and Angelina Jolie were together for more than a decade. Did you know that the movie that brought "Brangelina" together was filmed in Colorado?

The 2005 film *Mr. and Mrs. Smith* included scenes from numerous locations. The locations filmed in the desert, which featured Brad Pitt driving a dune-buggy, were filmed in Colorado. The scenes were filmed in Glenwood Canyon.

Though the celebrity couple has since divorced, it's crazy to think that if it weren't for this movie, there might never have been "Brangelina" at all. In fact, there's a good chance that we might never have begun to call couples by a combination of their names at all if it weren't for Brangelina filming *Mr. and Mrs. Smith* together in the first place.

Tim Allen Was Born in Colorado

Today, he's most well-known for his roles as a TV dad and for his famous role in Disney's *The Santa Clause* movie franchise. Did you know that actor Tim Allen was born in Colorado?

Tim Allen was born and raised in Denver, Colorado. Allen spent some of his childhood living in the city, but Allen's mother moved him and his five siblings to Birmingham, Michigan after his father died in a tragic car accident when he was 11 years old.

Tim Allen's career started out as a dare from his friends, which led him to participate in a comedy night at Mark Ridley's Comedy Castle in Royal Oak, Michigan. Allen began to do TV commercials and appeared on cable comedy shows, including Gary Thison's *Some Semblance of Sanity*.

In 1978, however, Allen's life took a turn when he was arrested for possessing more than 650 grams of cocaine at the Kalamazoo/Battle Creek International Airport. Allen made a plea bargain and spent two years and four months in prison.

Once he was released from prison, Tim Allen moved to Los Angeles and began to perform at The Comedy Store. Allen did stand-up performances for late-night talk shows.

Tim Allen's career took off in 1991 when he first appeared in the role of Tim "The Tool-Man" Taylor in the ABC sitcom *Home Improvement*. The show was produced by Wind Dancer Productions, which Allen and producer Carmen Finestra co-founded. The show ran until 1999. Allen earned $1.25 million an episode.

In 1994, Tim Allen played the lead role of Scott Calvin/Santa Claus in the Disney film, *The Santa Clause*. *The Santa Clause* was the highest-grossest film of the year. That same week, Allen's book *Don't Stand Too Close to a Naked Man* hit No. 1 on the *New York Times* best-seller list.

The Santa Clause was just the beginning of Allen's success as an actor for Disney. He also went on to do the voice of Buzz Lightyear in the Disney/Pixar animated films *Toy Story* and *Toy Story 2* and also starred in the Disney films *Jungle 2 Jungle* and *The Shaggy Dog*.

Tim Allen also became known for his holiday movie roles. After *The Santa Clause,* Allen later went on to play Scott Calvin in *The Clause 2* and eventually *The Santa Clause 3*. He also played Luther Krank in the film *Christmas with the Kranks,* which he starred in alongside Jamie Lee Curtis.

Tim Allen also played in seven seasons of the sitcom *Last Man Standing,* which ABC canceled during the sixth season when Allen made conservative comments. The seventh and final season was later picked up by FOX.

From famed TV dad to one of the most comical Santa Claus's of all-time, it's crazy to think it all started out in Denver.

Allen's *Home Improvement* Co-Star is Also from the State

Zachery Ty Bryan played Tim Allen's son Brad on *Home Improvement*. Did you know that Bryan was from Aurora, Colorado?

Before he landed his role in *Home Improvement,* Bryan was featured in a number of local print and TV advertisements in the Denver area. He later was featured in a showcase in New York City, which was he caught the eye of a professional talent representative. Bryan's interest as an actor led him to California, where he earned the role of Tim Allen's oldest son, despite being one month younger than Jonathan Taylor Thomas, who played the youngest son, Randy, on the show.

Some of Zachery Ty Bryan's other roles included Gomer in *The Fresh Prince of Bel-Air*, Peter Nichols in *Buffy the Vampire Slayer*, Caz Truman in *Veronica Mars*, and Scott Natterson in *Shark*. Since then, Bryan has had a number of guest roles, including in *Cold Case* and *Burn Notice*. But he'll always be most remembered for his role alongside fellow Coloradan Tim Allen.

This Jim Carrey Movie Was Filmed in the State

Today, it's one of the most well-known '90s movies of all-time. But did you know that the 1994 movie *Dumb and Dumber* was filmed in various locations throughout the state of Colorado?

The movie is about two friends who travel cross-country to Aspen, Colorado, with the goal of returning a briefcase of money to its owner.

Although some scenes from the movie were filmed in Utah and Rhode Island, there were a number of scenes that were actually filmed in Colorado. The town of Breckenridge, Colorado was used for some of the scenes that were supposed to take place in Aspen, CO.

The Stanley Hotel in Estes Park, Colorado acted as the fictional hotel, the Danbury Hotel, in the film. This is where the bar and staircase scenes were shot. The scenes in the snow, however, were shot at Copper Mountain Resort in Summit County, CO.

Some scenes from the movie were also filmed in Fort Morgan, Colorado. Some of these scenes include the truck stop, Sea Bass Diner, and the two-lane country road scenes.

Dumb and Dumber, which has somewhat of a cult following, is one of the most successful movie franchises to have ever been filmed in Colorado!

This *Sex and the City* Star Hails from Colorado

Did you know that *Sex and the City* actress Kristin Davis is from Colorado?

The actress behind the character of Charlotte York Goldenblatt on the beloved HBO series was born in Boulder, Colorado. Her family later moved to Columbia, South Carolina.

Davis had aspirations of being an actress from the age of 9. One of her first performances was in *Snow White and the Seven Dwarfs.*

After graduating from Rutgers University in New Jersey, Davis moved to New York City where she was a waitress. She and a friend later opened a yoga studio. During the early 1990s, she acted in a couple of shows on *General Hospital*. In 1995, the actress's big break came when she earned the role of Brooke Armstrong Campbell in the show *Melrose Place*. The producers killed off Davis's character after a year. Davis also played in episodes of *Friends, Seinfeld*, and *Will and Grace*.

In 1998, Kristin Davis earned the role of Charlotte on *Sex and the City*. She remained an important cast member until the show ended in 2004. Davis earned an Emmy nomination in 2004 for her portrayal of Charlotte during the show's last season.

Davis resumed her role as Charlotte in the films *Sex and the City* in 2008 and *Sex and the City 2* in 2010.

The actress has also starred in a number of films, including *The Adventures of Sharkboy and Lavagirl in 3D, The Shaggy Dog, Deck the Halls,* and *Couples Retreat*.

And to think that it all started out in Boulder, Colorado.

This Cult Favorite Christmas Movie Was Filmed in the State

Today, it's one of the most popular Christmas movies of all-time. Did you know that *National Lampoon's Christmas Vacation* was filmed in Colorado?

The 1989 film, which has a cult-like following, opens with a scene as the Griswold family searches for the perfect Christmas tree. The scene was filmed at the Breckenridge Golf Course in Breckenridge, Colorado. Locals were used as extras for the scene.

There's also a sledding scene in the movie that was filmed at Breckenridge Ski Resort on Peak 8.

Scenes from the movie, which featured Chevy Chase, were also shot in Silverthorne and Frisco, Colorado. There's a scene in the film where Clark and "Cousin Eddie" are shopping at Wal-Mart in the film. This scene was filmed at the Wal-Mart in Frisco, Colorado.

Not every scene was filmed in the Centennial State, however. The set of the Griswold family's house and the street they live on is actually located in Burbank, California.

Stephen King's *The Shining* Was Inspired by This Colorado Hotel

Did you know that Stephen King's *The Shining* was inspired by a famously haunted hotel in Colorado?

The Stanley Hotel is more than 100 years old and is said to be home to a number of unexplained paranormal occurrences. King got to experience this himself when he and his wife Tabitha spent the night in room 217 when the hotel was empty because it was getting ready to close for the winter season.

King had been struggling with the book, which he had already started. At that time, the book's working title was *Darkshine* and was set in an amusement park. However, King wanted a more isolated setting.

Stephen King was inspired by the Stanley's remoteness, large size, and eerie desolation. When he went into the bathroom, he imagined the possibility of someone dying in the claw foot tub. That was the moment he knew that a hotel would work for the setting of his book. Thus, the Stanley became the inspiration of the Overlook Hotel in *The Shining*.

The hotel in the book is located in the fictional town of Sidewinder, Colorado, which is supposed to be located near Estes Park. Room 217—the same number of the room King himself stayed in at the Stanley—is featured in the book. While King doesn't mention the Stanley in the book, he has talked about it being the inspiration behind the Overlook Hotel in various interviews. being the inspiration behind the Overlook Hotel in various interviews. being the inspiration behind the Overlook Hotel in various interviews.

Today, Room 217 is the most requested room at the Stanley Hotel.

The Shining was published in 1977 and became King's 3rd best-selling novel.

You might be disappointed to learn that the Stanley Hotel was not featured in the film adaptation of *The*

Shining. The Stanley was, however, featured in *The Shining* mini-series.

The Fray Was Formed in Denver

Did you know that the rock band The Fray was formed in Denver, Colorado?

The band was started back in 2002 by Isaac Slade and Joe King, who attended Faith Christian Academy in Arvada, CO together. They reconnected after graduation and started to write songs together. They later added guitarist Mike Ayars and drummer Zach Johnson. Isaac Slade's younger brother Caleb also joined as a bassist, but he was later asked to leave. Isaac's rocky relationship with Caleb became the inspiration of the song "Over My Head (Cable Car)." Zach Johnson later left the band as well.

Ben Wysocki, who was a few years behind Isaac Slade and Joe King at Faith Christian Academy, later joined as a drummer for the band. Dave Welsh, who previously been in a band with Slade and Wysocki, also joined the band as its lead guitarist. It's at this time that they chose the name "The Fray" for their band. They came up with the name after they asked people to write down potential names for them to choose from. The band said they chose the name because they often argued about the lyrics in their songs.

The Fray's debut album, *How to Save a Life*, was successful. Their first single "Over My Head (Cable Car)" became a top 10 hit in the U.S. Their second single, "How to Save a Life," hit No. 3 on the *Billboard* Hot 100 and brought the band international fame.

The band's second, self-titled album, which was released in 2009, hit No. 1 on the *Billboard* Hot 100 charts. It was also nominated for a Grammy Award in 2010.

And to think that it all started out with schoolmates in Arvada, Colorado!

This Famous Cartoonist Lived in Colorado

Did you know that one of the most famous comic strip cartoonists of all time once lived in Colorado?

Charles Schulz is most well-known for being the creator and cartoonist of the famous comic strip *Peanuts*, which features beloved characters Charlie Brown and Snoopy. Did you know that the cartoonist once lived in the Colorado Springs area?

During the 1950s, Schulz resided in the Centennial State. He even painted a *Peanuts* mural on the wall of his daughter's nursery. (Today, that wall can be found at the Charles Schulz Museum in Santa Rosa, California).

What you might not know is that two characters from the famous comic strip actually originated from

Colorado Springs. When Schulz was living in the area, he had neighbors with the surname Van Pelt. The couple had two children named Linus and Lucy, whose names were used as characters in *Peanuts*. Schulz has said that, aside from the name, the character of Lucy was actually based on his wife, however.

This Late Actress Filmed Her Show at the Air Force Academy

Did you know that episodes of Lucille Ball's show, *Here's Lucy*, were filmed at the Air Force Academy in Colorado Springs?

It was back in 1969 that the actress starred in the second season of *Here's Lucy*, which was filmed primarily on location at the Air Force Academy.

The actress might not be the most well-known for this show, but true Lucille Ball fans enjoyed her comedic genius in the series.

The Creators of This Animated TV Series are From Colorado

If you're a fan of the animated TV series *South Park*, then you probably already know the show is set in the fictional town of South Park, Colorado. But did you know that the show's creators are from the Centennial State?

Matt Stone and Trey Parker both hail from Colorado. Matt Stone grew up in Littleton, Colorado, where he attended Heritage High School. Trey Parker was born in Conifer, CO and attended Evergreen High School.

Matt Stone and Trey Parker met when they were taking a film class together at the University of Colorado Boulder. Stone and Parker not only co-write and co-direct *South Park*, but they also voice many of the show's characters.

The fictional town in the show is supposed to be located in the real South Park basin of the Rocky Mountains in central Colorado. The town's main street and other features are also based on the appearance of Fairplay, Colorado. *South Park* also features snowy Coloradan landscapes and real-life Coloradan landmarks.

This Controversial Actress's Career Started Out in the Centennial State

Did you know that comedian and actress Roseanne Barr's career started out in Colorado?

Barr was born and raised in Salt Lake City, Utah. After she dropped out of high school, she moved to Colorado. Though she was only a minor at the time, she did this by telling her parents she was going to visit a friend in Colorado for two weeks, but she never came back home. Instead, she moved to a hippie commune in the state.

Roseanne Barr later moved to Denver with her then husband and their three children.

She did stand-up comedy gigs in clubs throughout Denver and surrounding towns. She went on to audition at The Comedy Store in Los Angeles before later appearing on *The Tonight Show* in 1985. The following year, she performed on *Late Night with David Letterman* and on a Rodney Dangerfield Special.

In 1987, she was given an HBO special called *The Roseanne Barr Show*. During her routine, she popularized the term "domestic goddess," which referred to a housewife/homemaker.

Barr was later offered the role of Peg Bundy in the TV series *Married... with Children*. Barr turned the role down, however.

Her success led to ABC giving Barr a series of her own: *Roseanne*. The series aired from 1988 to 1977 and again in 2018. The series was extremely well received when it first debuted, beating out even *The Cosby Show*. The revival in 2018 saw 27.26 million viewers total.

While there's no doubt that Roseanne Barr has since become a controversial household name, it all started out with a girl who ran away to Colorado.

This *Gilmore Girls* Actress Hails from the State

Did you know that one of the *Gilmore Girls* actresses is from the Centennial State?

Actress Kelly Bishop, who's most well-known for her role as Emily Gilmore, was born in Colorado Springs. Bishop grew up in Denver, Colorado. There, she attended the San Jose Ballet School.

When Bishop was 18 years old, she moved to New York City, where she worked for a year-round ballet company at Radio City Music Hall. Bishop continued to perform as a dancer until she was cast in a Broadway production of *Golden Rainbow* in 1967.

The actress's big break came when she was cast as Sheila in *A Chorus Line* on Broadway.

Her big on-screen break came when she played Mrs. Houseman in *Dirty Dancing* in 1987. Although Bishop was originally cast in a smaller role in the film, she was recast when Lynne Lipton, who had originally been cast as Mrs. Houseman, became ill during shooting.

In 2000, Bishop appeared as Emily in the WB/CW series *Gilmore Girls*. The show ran for seven seasons, during which it gained somewhat of a cult following.

Bishop later reprised her role as Emily in the Netflix Original mini-series *Gilmore Girls: A Year in the Life* in 2016.

Although the actress is most well-known for her roles in *Gilmore Girls* and *Dirty Dancing*, she has played in a number of other roles. Some of these include *Miami Rhapsody*, *Blue Rhapsody*, and *Anything Goes*. Bishop also starred in the short-lived ABC Family show *Bunheads*, which was produced by *Gilmore Girls* creator Amy Sherman-Palladino.

This Late Singer Loved Colorado

Did you know that the late musician John Denver loved Colorado? In fact, it's the reason he chose the surname "Denver" for his stage name.

John Denver was born as Henry John Deutschendorf Jr. He was told that his last name wouldn't comfortably fit on a marquee, so he decided to adopt the surname "Denver." He chose it after the capital of his favorite state. Denver lived in Aspen, Colorado for most of his life.

He wrote numerous songs about his love of Colorado. One of the most popular songs he wrote about the state was "Rocky Mountain High," which was adopted by the Colorado state legislature as the state's second official song in 2007. Unfortunately, John Denver wasn't around when that happened. Denver, who was a pilot, died in an aircraft accident in 1997.

Over the course of his career, Denver released about 300 songs, with the most popular being "Take Me

Home, Country Roads," "Leaving on a Jet Plane," "Calypso," "Rocky Mountain High," "Sunshine on My Shoulders," "Thank God I'm a Country Boy," and "Annie's Song."

This Netflix Original Series Takes Place in Colorado

Did you know that the Netflix Original series *The Ranch* is set in Colorado?

The show, which stars Ashton Kutcher, is set in a fictional town called Garrison, CO on the also fictitious Iron River Ranch.

It might disappoint you to learn that most of the show isn't filmed in Colorado. Although the opening scenes of the show feature Ouray and Norwood, Colorado, the majority of the show is not filmed in the Centennial State. So, where is it really filmed?

The Ranch is actually filmed on a sound stage in Burbank, California. It's filmed in front of a live audience.

RANDOM FACTS

1. *Fast & Furious 7* was filmed in Colorado. The film, which is the last movie of the film franchise that features Paul Walker, has a scene that was filmed at Pikes Peak and Monarch Pass.

2. The 1989 film *Indiana Jones and the Last Crusade* was filmed in several Colorado locations, including Pagosa Springs, Cortez, and Alamosa. The film also features the Cumbres & Toltec Railroad in Antonito, CO.

3. Actor Bill Murray is most well-known for the films *Groundhog Day* and *Ghostbusters*. Before he became an actor, however, Murray first attended Regis University in Denver, Colorado. The actor, who was enrolled in the pre-med program, dropped out.

4. The late actress Amanda Peterson was born in Greeley, Colorado. Most will remember Peterson for her beloved role as Cindy Mancini in the movie *Can't Buy Me Love*. Peterson passed away in 2016.

5. *Catch and Release* is set in the city of Boulder, Colorado. Starring Jennifer Gardner and Timothy Olyphant, some of the movie was filmed on

location in Boulder. Several Boulder locations, including the Pearl Street Mall, are featured in the 2006 film.

6. Actor Kevin Costner owns a 165-acre ranch near Aspen, Colorado. It has been said that the actor loves his ranch so much that he intends to be buried there.

7. The late 70s/early 80s show *Mork & Mindy* was set in Boulder, Colorado. It might surprise you to learn that most of the show, which starred Robin Williams, actually was *not* filmed on location. However, the exterior shots of Mindy's house were taken at 1619 in Boulder, Colorado.

8. The 2013 Disney film *The Lone Ranger*, which starred Johnny Depp, features mostly desert. Almost the entire movie was filmed in Creede, Colorado.

9. Jesse Carmichael, Maroon 5's keyboardist and rhythm guitar player, was born in Boulder, Colorado. Carmichael originally began playing the guitar in junior high. It wasn't until college that he started playing the keyboards, which he is most well-known for the today. Carmichael was one of the founding members of Maroon 5's first band, Kara's Flowers.

10. Ace Young, who was on the 5th season of *American Idol*, is from Denver, Colorado.

11. Actress Jessica Biel grew up in Boulder, Colorado. The actress, who's probably most well-known for her marriage to Justin Timberlake, got her big break as Mary Camden in the TV series *7th Heaven.*

12. On *7th Heaven* Mary Camden's love interest, Ben Kinkirk, was played by actor Geoffrey Manton. The actor was raised in Green Mountain Falls, Colorado. And he's not the only one. His onset brother, Kevin Kinkirk, was played by George Stults—who just so happens to be Manton's brother in real life.

13. Spencer Smith, who was the co-founder and former drummer of the band Panic! at the Disco, was born in Denver. Smith left the band after four records. He now works as a manager and talent finder at DCD2 Records, which is owned by Patrick Stump and Pete Wentz of Fall Out Boy.

14. Actress Amy Adams was raised in Castle Rock, Colorado from the age of eight. The actress's first performance was as a dancer in *A Chorus Line* production at a dinner theater in Boulder, CO. Though Adams is most well-known for her role in the Disney film *Enchanted*, her first major role was in *Catch Me If You Can* alongside Leonardo DiCaprio.

15. Actor John Lynch played Drew Carey's brother in *The Drew Carey Show*. He's also well-known for his role as Twisty the Clown in *American Horror Story: Freak Show* and *American Horror Story: Cult*. Lynch is from Boulder, Colorado and went to Regis Jesuit High School in Denver, CO.

16. The late actress Connie Sawyer was from Pueblo, Colorado. Sawyer, who has been given the nickname "The Clown Princess of Comedy," played in a number of films, including *When Harry Met Sally...*, *Dumb and Dumber*, and *Pineapple Express.*

17. Jon Heder is best recognized for his lead role in the comedic film *Napoleon Dynamite*. Heder was born in Fort Collins, Colorado, though his family later relocated to Oregon. In addition to playing Napoleon Dynamite, Heder also played in *The Benchwarmers*, *When in Rome*, and *Blades of Glory.*

18. Actress Katie Leclerc was raised in Lakewood, Colorado. Leclerc is most well-known for her role as a deaf teenager named Daphne Vasquez in *Switched at Birth*. Leclerc has Ménière's disease, which causes hearing loss. Although Leclerc was hard of hearing (rather than deaf) when the show was being recorded, the actress put on a fake deaf accent for the role.

19. Actress Keri Russell, who's best-known for her role as Felicity Porter in the WB TV series *Felicity*,

has starred in a number of movies. Some of these include *August Rush*, *Waitress*, *Dawn of the Planet of the Apes*, and *Mission: Impossible III*. Russell spent some of her childhood in Highlands Ranch, Colorado, though the family moved often for her father's job.

20. Actor/filmmaker Scott Takeda attended the University of Colorado in Boulder. Takeda has played in films including *Dallas Buys Club* and *Gone Girl*.

Test Yourself – Questions

1. Which *Home Improvement* actor is not from Colorado?

   a. Tim Allen
   b. Jonathan Taylor Thomas
   c. Zachery Ty Bryan

2. Which actress was born in Colorado?

   a. Lucille Ball
   b. Roseanne Barr
   c. Kelly Bishop

3. The co-creators of *South Park* met when they were taking which type of class at the University of Colorado Boulder?

   a. Writing
   b. Film
   c. Graphic arts

4. Stephen King's book *The Shining* was based on which hotel?

   a. The Overlook Hotel
   b. The Stanley Hotel
   c. The Cliff House at Pikes Peak

5. The band The Fray was formed in which Colorado city?

   a. Boulder
   b. Colorado Springs
   c. Denver

Answers

1. b.

2. c.

3. a.

4. b.

5. c.

CHAPTER THREE

COLORADO'S INVENTIONS, IDEAS, AND MORE

Have you ever given any thought to what inventions have come from Colorado? Do you know which famous foods have started out in the state? Do you know about the ice cream treat that was invented in the Centennial State? Do you know which Mexican food chain started out in Colorado? One hint: It's not Taco Bell. Do you know which widespread holiday tradition started out rather tragically in the Centennial State? To find out the answers to these questions and learn about other products, companies, and inventions that started out in Colorado, read on!

The Cheeseburger

The average American eats three burgers each week. This means that nearly 50 billion burgers are consumed in the United States on a yearly basis. Have you ever wondered who to credit with the invention?

Let's get something straight first: this is not the invention of the *hamburger*, which was actually invented by a Danish immigrant named Louis Lassen who was working in New Haven, Connecticut. But who thought to add cheese to a hamburger, forever changing the way people across the entire U.S. enjoy burgers?

A number of chefs have tried to take credit for being the first to ever invent a hamburger with cheese, but it turns out that it was actually a Coloradan named Louis Ballast who came up with the idea.

Although this is highly controversial, we accept this as the truth because Louis Ballast, who owned the Humpty Dumpty Drive-In in Denver, was awarded a Food Trademark for the word "cheeseburger" back in 1935. Today, there's also a monument in Ballast's honor where the Humpty Dumpty once stood at 2776 N. Speer Boulevard in Denver.

Even though Ballast had the name of his creation trademarked, he never actually enforced it because restaurants all across America soon began to sell cheeseburgers. However, Ballast did hang a sign in his restaurant, calling it "Home of the Original Cheeseburger."

Tampons

Have you ever wondered who to thank for the invention of tampons? Well, it turns out that Tampax was invented in the Centennial State.

Dr. Earle Haas had a goal to invent something better than the "rags" his wife had to wear. The idea came to him after a friend in California used a sponge in her vagina to absorb her menstrual flow.

Haas designed a plug of cotton that had to inserted with two cardboard tubes. He didn't want women to have to touch the cotton.

His patent, which he filed as the "Catamenial device," was granted in September of 1933.

It might surprise you to learn that Dr. Haas didn't have luck getting interest in the invention. Even the Johnson & Johnson company wasn't interested.

In October of 1933, Haas sold his patent and trademark to a Denver businesswoman by the name of Gertrude Tendrich. His invention earned him $32,000 (or the equivalent of more than $600,000 in 2019).

Gertrude Tendrich started the Tampax company, of which she was the first president. Tendrich made the first Tampax tampons at home with her sewing machine, as well as with Dr. Haas's compression machine.

The first Tampax tampons were sold in the U.S. in 1936.

After selling the rights to the tampon, he continued with his doctor's practice and various business enterprises. He later regretted selling the rights but was glad it was successful, and died at 93 in 1981. Up to right before his death he continued to try to improve the tampon.

Western Omelet

Did you know that the Western omelet is sometimes called a Denver omelet? This is because the omelet actually originated from the Mile High City.

Also known as a Southwest omelet (since it's often served in the Southwestern U.S.), the omelet is generally filled with diced ham, green bell peppers, and onions. Sometimes, the omelet is made of egg whites, but other times, it may be made from whole eggs. The omelet is also sometimes topped with cheese and is generally served with hash browns or fried potatoes.

Where did the omelet originate from? Well, that's actually not *entirely* known for sure. But here's what we do know:

The Denver omelet originally started out as a Denver Sandwich. Although the sandwich originated in Denver, it was pretty popular throughout the entire

U.S. during the 1950s. The Denver Sandwich, by the way, is essentially a Denver omelet served between two slices of toast. Therefore, it's safe to credit whoever came up with the idea of the Denver sandwich as the inventor of the Denver omelet, too — but no one knows who that is for sure.

There are several theories about who may have invented the Denver sandwich. According to one story, an Italian immigrant sold the sandwiches from a Denver street cart in the early 1890s. There has been a theory about pioneer women inventing the sandwich to mask the taste of spoiled eggs with onions. Some have questioned if Chinese immigrants may have modified egg foo young to provide food to laborers on the transcontinental railroad. Denver restaurateurs M.D. Looney and Albert A. McVittie have both taken claim to the invention in 1907. It's also been rumored to have been invented at Tabor Hotel in Denver.

Whoever invented the Western omelet, it's safe to say that it was created in Denver *and* it's delicious.

Root Beer Float

Did you know that one of America's favorite ice cream treats was invented in Colorado? The root beer float was created in Cripple Creek, Colorado!

Frank Wisner, who owned the Cripple Creek Cow Mountain Gold Mining Company, was allegedly looking out his window one night. He was thinking about his line of soda waters and noticed the way the full moon shone against the snow-capped Cow Mountain. It reminded him of vanilla ice cream.

Wisner went back to the bar and added a scoop of ice cream to Myers Avenue Red Rot Beer, which was a favorite among children. He tried his concoction and liked it.

The next day, he began to serve his invention to people who came into the restaurant. It turned out to be an instant success.

Although Wisner called his invention the "Black Cow Mountain," the children shortened the beverage's name to the "Black Cow."

Today, thousands of root beer floats are enjoyed in the United States every day. And this isn't even to mention the many root beer float-inspired food items, ranging from Luigi's and Rita's Italian ice to marshmallow Peeps. And it all started out in Cripple Creek, Colorado.

Jolly Ranchers

They're one of America's favorite hard candies, but did you know that Jolly Ranchers were invented by a Colorado native?

Bill Harmsen, who was from Golden, CO, invented the candy back in 1949. He and his wife, Dorothy, founded the Jolly Rancher Company in 1949. They chose the name "Jolly Rancher" because they wanted it to seem like a friendly western company.

Although Harmsen and his wife tried to sell ice cream first, they quickly realized that it wasn't an easy sell during the cold months. They began to sell hard candies, which turned out to be a success. Harmsen began to focus more on the candies, since they could be enjoyed the entire year, regardless of the temperature.

The first Jolly Rancher flavors included grape, watermelon, Fire Stix, and apple.

Today, the Jolly Rancher line of candies is owned by Hershey's.

Chipotle Mexican Grill

It's a favorite fast food chain among many. Did you know that Chipotle Mexican Grill started out in Denver?

The fast-food chain was founded by University of Colorado Boulder alumni Steve Ells back in 1993. Ells opened the first Chipotle near the University of Denver campus.

Ells and his father figured out that the restaurant would need to sell approximately 107 burritos every day in order for it to be successful. Within a month, Chipotle was selling more than 1,000 burritos a day.

By 1998, there were 16 Chipotle locations in Colorado. That year, McDonald's invested in the chain. With McDonald's as an investor, Chipotle grew to more than 500 locations. In 2006, however, McDonald's ended its relationship with Chipotle.

Chipotle is perhaps most well-known as being pioneers for the clean fast-food movement. The chain uses more naturally-raised meat than any other chain in the U.S. It also uses organic and local ingredients whenever possible. Chipotle is also considered to be one of the healthiest fast food chains in the country.

The name "Chipotle" comes from the Mexican/Nahuatl word for a dried and smoked jalapeño popper—even though the chain doesn't serve jalapeño poppers.

Coors Beer

If you read the first chapter, then you already know that Colorado is a big beer state. The Centennial State is home to a number of microbreweries, as well as well-known beers. Although a lot of great breweries are located in Colorado, Coors is, by far, the most famous beer that hails from the state!

Production of Coors beer started out in 1873 when two German immigrants by the names of Adolph Coors and Jacob Schueler opened a brewery in Golden, Colorado. They bought a Pilsner-style beer recipe from a Czech immigrant. In order to balance out the yeasty flavor, they used mountain spring water.

Although Schueler initially had an $18,000 stake in the brewery, Coors eventually bought him out in 1880.

The company was affected by the Prohibition. Colorado was one of the first states to initiate the Prohibition, which began in the state in 1916. The rest of the country followed suit in 1920.

Adolph Coors and his sons had several other businesses, however, which allowed the brewery to survive this rough time. During the prohibition, Coors was able to stay in business by brewing malted milk and "near beer," which contained little to no alcohol.

By the end of the Prohibition, Coors was one of the few breweries that managed to survive.

Tragically, Adolph Coors did not survive the Prohibition. In 1929, Coors allegedly committed suicide by jumping out of a window in Virginia Beach. Coors, who was 82 years old at the time of his death, was believed to have killed himself due to depression over the effect the Prohibition had taken on his business. Some believed that Coors had actually been pushed out the window, however.

In 2007, Coors merged with SABMiller to form MillerCoors, making it the 2nd largest brewer in America, as well as the 6th largest brewer in the entire world. The MillerCoors Golden Brewery is also the No. 1 largest single-site brewery in the world.

Today, MillerCoors produces 30% of the beer that's sold in America. In addition to Coors and Coors Light, the company also produces Miller Lite, Miller High Life, Miller Genuine Draft, Blue Moon, Molson Canadian, Hamm's, and Crispin Hard Cider.

In case you're wondering, the mountains that are featured on the Coors Lights can are real. Well, *sort of*. The mountains on the can are based on Wilson Peak in the San Juan Mountains, which is located approximately 11 miles from Telluride Ski Resort.

The next time you're in Colorado, you even take a tour of the Coors Brewery. The Coors Brewery Tour preserves the brewer's history and helps you learn more about the beer-making and packaging processes. The tour also features a number of historical artifacts and memorabilia.

Once the tour is over, you can sample beer from the Hospitality Lounge and check out the Coors & Co. gift shop, where you'll find merchandise featuring Coors, as well as Colored-themed merch.

Outdoor Christmas Lights

For many of us, stringing our outdoor Christmas lights puts us in the holiday spirit. Going out to see outdoor Christmas lights is also a favorite American pastime. But did you know that the tradition of outdoor Christmas lights started out in Denver, Colorado in the early 1900s? It all came about due to one father's attempt at cheering up his son during the holiday.

The story is actually a pretty tragic one, and it goes like this:

On Christmas Eve in 1914, a 10-year-old boy named David Jonathan Sturgeon was laying in bed at his family's home at 4408 West 34th Avenue. Sturgeon was too sick to join his family for the celebration around the Christmas tree.

David's father, David Dwight "D.D." Sturgeon, was an electrician. Wanting his sick son to feel included in the holiday festivities, D.D. Sturgeon dipped lightbulbs in red and green paint and connected them to an electrical wire. He then hung the lights in a pine tree outside his son's window. Not only did Sturgeon cheer up the young David, but people came from miles away to see the invention. It was the first outdoor Christmas tree to ever be lit with lights.

The following Christmas, Sturgeon's neighbors decided to decorate their outdoor lights, too.

Tragically, Sturgeon's son was not around to see it, as he died from another illness.

The tradition of the outdoor Christmas lights lived on, however. Soon enough, Denver had gained recognition for outdoor Christmas lights.

In 1918, the country's first outdoor lighting contest was held in Denver. Hundreds of people entered.

The following year, John Malpiede, who was the official city electrician, replaced the lights in Denver Civic Center with red and green globes for the holiday season. In 2020, Malpiede put a lit outdoor Christmas tree in front of the State Capitol.

By the late 1920s, Denver had gained the nickname of the "Christmas Capital of the World."

In 1945, the NBC network broadcasted a tribute to Denver, thanking the Sturgeon family for the holiday tradition they had created.

D.D. Sturgeon was nicknamed the "Father of Yule Lighting". The company he founded, Sturgeon Electric, is still around today—and they continue to perform greatness. In 2018, the company surprised a Colorado Springs 8-year-old leukemia patient and his family with a decorated home of more than 3,000 lights in 2018.

Crocs

Some people consider them the most hideous shoes ever made. Others consider them to be the most comfortable shoes ever made. Whether you love them or hate them, Crocs were invented in Boulder, Colorado!

Crocs were founded by Scott Seamans, George Boedecker, Jr. and Lyndon "Duke" Hanson. They acquired the design from a company called Foam Creations. Crocs bought exclusive rights to the company and their manufacturing operations to ensure exclusive rights to the foam resin known as Croslite that's used in the design. The material is known as an injection-molded EVA foam, which forms to the feet of the person wearing it. According to many podiatrists, Crocs offer health benefits to those who wear them.

The first Crocs model, which was called the *Beach*, was meant to be a boating shoe. It first made its debut at the Fort Lauderdale Boat Show, where it sold out all 200 pairs that were produced at the time.

To date, 300 million pairs of Crocs have been sold. And it all started out in Boulder!

Shredded Wheat

Shredded wheat is an important American breakfast staple. Have you ever wondered who invented shredded wheat? The credit goes to Henry Perky, who was a native of Denver, Colorado.

In 1890, Perky developed a method of processing wheat into strips.

Perky's process went like this: The strips were formed into pillow-like biscuits and then tempered, so that moisture is able to evenly diffuse into the grain. The grain then moves through rollers that had grooves on one side, producing strands of shredded wheat. Groups of strands were stacked together. Moist stacks of strands would then be crimped periodically to produce individual pieces of shredded wheat. The cereal pieces then went into an oven and were baked until their moisture content was decreased to 5%.

Perky's shredded wheat cereal was first sold to vegetarian restaurants in 1892.

Perky's invention sparked the interest of Dr. John Harvey Kellogg, the inventor of corn flakes. Kellogg offered to buy Perky's patent in 1906, but his offer was too low.

Nabisco went on to purchase his recipe in 1928.

Shopping Centers

Today, we take shopping centers for granted. Have you ever given any thought to where they got their start? Did you know that the idea of shopping centers actually originated from Denver?

Denver architect Temple Buell came up with the idea back in the 1920s when he began to design the Cherry Creek Shopping, which was opened in 1951. He was the first one to come up with the concept of indoor/outdoor retail developments, paving the way for shopping centers across America.

For his invention, Temple Buell was dubbed the nickname of "Father of the Shopping Mall."

Quiznos

Quiznos is a well-known fast food sub shop in America. Did you know the first Quiznos restaurant was opened in 1981 in Denver, Colorado? It was co-founded by Jimmy Lambatos and Todd Disner.

The sandwich shop grew popular thanks to its toasted subs, which were inspired by the oven-baked sandwiches that Lambatos ate while growing up in New York. Toasted subs had been unheard of in Colorado when Quiznos first opened.

By 1983, Quiznos began to offer franchises.

Wondering where the name "Quiznos" came from? It was a faux Italian surname that Jimmy Lambatos came up with. When he came up with the name, his goal was to incorporate what he believed to be two of the most memorable letters of the alphabet. Apparently, the name worked for him... at least at one point in time.

Quiznos ended up filing for bankruptcy in 2014 and was acquired by a California-based company called High Bluff Capital Partners in 2018. Despite the change of hands, the company's headquarters remain in Denver, Colorado.

As of 2018, Quiznos had 800 locations. As of 2016, it's the 9th largest sub chain in North America—though it used to rank No. 2 and once had almost 5,000 locations.

Smashburger

Today, it's a well-known hamburger restaurant chain. Did you know that Smashburger started out in Colorado?

The company was founded by Tom Ryan (who created stuffed crust pizza for Pizza Hut and also worked as chief concept officer for McDonald's) and David Prokupek (a previous owner of Quiznos). Their goal was simple: to create a higher market for hamburgers with a "better burger" concept in mind.

Ryan and Prokupek bought Icon Burger, which was a restaurant in Denver. They wanted to experiment with cooking techniques and managing a higher-end burger restaurant. They spent six months making improvements to the restaurant's kitchen in order to ensure that Smashburger would run as efficiently as possible. Their kitchen concept was later adopted and became the standardized kitchen at every Smashburger restaurant. It consisted of using flattop grills for the kitchen rather than barbecue grills or char broils.

The restaurant used a "smashing" technique, which is done with a special cutter and technique. This allows new cooks to undergo fast training.

While burgers may be what the chain is most famous for, they aren't the only thing you'll find on the menu at Smashburger. The menu also includes chicken, turkey, and portobello sandwiches, as well as fries, sweet potato fries, and appetizers.

Ryan and Prokupek also did a blind taste test of 300 different types of beef before they chose chopped Angus beef. They narrowed down the options until they were down to four and discovered all four were Angus beef that had been provided by different distributors.

As of 2018, there were 370 Smashburger locations in 37 U.S. states and 9 countries.

Ibotta

Today, Ibotta is one of the most popular ways to save money. It's often featured on a lot of menu-saving blogs and is a favorite among "mommy bloggers." The app has grown in popularity since people have developed an obsession with extreme couponing and cashback. Some people even earn hundreds of dollars back in cash from the app a month.

Have you ever wondered who was the brains of the popular smartphone cash back app? As it turns out, you can thank a Denver native for inventing Ibotta.

Founded by Bryan Leach, Ibotta was incorporated in 2011. Leach came up with the idea when he realized that there was a need for a more innovative way of connecting consumers with brands and retailers through smartphone technology. Leach wanted to provide tech-savvy consumers with a way that they could easily earn cashback on the items they purchased every day.

The company partners with companies to offer rebates and discounts on a number of types of purchases. It also offers alcohol cashback and rebates, which can be used at liquor/grocery stores, restaurants, and bars. For this reason, Ibotta users have to be 21 years of age or older to use the app, even if they don't plan to purchase beer or wine.

As of 2016, the Ibotta app was only available in the United States and works on both iOS and Android devices. That year, the app claimed to work at over 500,000 locations.

As of 2019, the company has paid more than $375 million in cash back.

Hammond's Candies

Most well-known for their colorful lollipops and ribbon candies, Hammond's Candies was started in Denver, Colorado.

In 1920, Carl Hammond's mom told him he could leave school if he entered a trade. This prompted him to find a gig as an apprentice for a candy maker. He later went on to open his own shop.

Seventy years later, Williams-Sonoma wanted to sell Hammond's toffee. It was at this time that the candy corner shop turned into a major manufacturer.

In 2007, Hammond's was acquired by Andrew Schuman.

Today, Hammond's is the largest manufacturer of handmade confections in America.

Hammond's Candies is most well-known for its oversized candy canes, lollipops, and ribbon candies. It also makes chocolates, hard candies, and more. And it all started out with one boy's desire to leave school!

RANDOM FACTS

1. Rumor has it that the teddy bear *may* have been invented by maids at the Hotel Colorado when President Teddy Roosevelt was staying there during a hunting trip. However, this is quite controversial. There have been other claims as to who actually invented the toy. This is just one popular legend about the teddy bear's invention that cannot be confirmed.

2. The helicopter prototype was invented in the Centennial State. In 1909, John Milton Cage, Sr., who was a Denver native, worked on an early version of a helicopter. He was living in Capitol Hill at the time. Cage later moved to Los Angeles and went on to develop new submarines.

3. The parking boot was invented in Denver. Back in the 1940s, getting a parking ticket meant you would be towed. A Colorado Symphony violinist by the name of Frank Marugg designed the wheel clamp, which is otherwise known as the parking boot or Denver boot, in 1944. Today his invention is on display at the Smithsonian.

4. Celestial Seasonings Tea got its start in Boulder, Colorado. It all started back in 1969 when a group of young entrepreneurs' hand-harvested

fresh herbs from the Rocky Mountains. They packaged the herbs into hand-sewn muslin bags, which they later sold at local health food stores. Today, Celestial Seasonings Tea is one of the largest specialty tea manufacturers in the United States and sells more than 1.6 million cups of tea each year. Ingredients are also no longer limited to the Rocky Mountains and instead come from more than 35 countries. You can take the company's tea tour and check out its infamous "peppermint room" when you visit Boulder.

5. OtterBox produces water-proof, shock-proof, and drop-proof cell phone cases. The company is based in Fort Collins, Colorado. It was founded in 1991 by Curt Richardson, who made his first "Otterbox" in his garage. Richardson came up with the idea due to the rise in popularity of water sports. By 2004, OtterBox had begun to sell iPod cases. Though the company no longer produces iPod cases, it does make cases for cell phones and other technologies from Apple, Amazon, Blackberry, Samsung, Google, LG, and other companies. Today, the company also offers accessories to protect military technology.

6. Noosa Yogurt was invented by a Colorado resident named Koel Thomae. Thomae was visiting Queensland, Australia back in 2005 when she came across a yogurt shop that served yogurt

with a unique flavor. A couple of years later, Thomae saw a flyer for a family-owned dairy farm. She called the farm owner, Rob Graves, and persuaded him to be her business partner. Noosa quickly ended up in Whole Foods and eventually Target. Today, Noosa is known for its extremely creamy texture and its unique flavorings, such as Blackberry Serrano and Raspberry Lemonade.

7. Scott's Liquid Gold started out in Denver, Colorado. In 1951, Ida Goldstein started the company in her garage, where she and her three sons mixed batches of the wood cleaner. Today, Ida's son Mark is the President and CEO of Scott's Liquid Gold. The company remains in Denver, Colorado.

8. Bhakti, which one of the top brands of chai, was founded by a Boulder native. It was founded by Brook Eddy, who took a trip to India and was intrigued by the ritual of drinking chai tea. She started brewing her own chai when she returned to Boulder. The single mom of twins quit her job to start Bhakti.

9. Mexican hamburgers can be found at many restaurants throughout Colorado, but the burger was invented at Joe's Buffet, which was located in Denver before it closed. A Mexican hamburger is basically a burrito with a burger in it. A

Mexican burger is a tortilla filled with refried beans, your choice of meat, a hamburger patty, and green Chile. You can find it at both Mexican and non-Mexican restaurants throughout the state, especially in Denver.

10. Rudi's Organic Bakery was founded in Denver. The company is known for its healthy, preservative-free bread, rolls, and buns.

11. Corepower Yoga was founded by Trevor Tice in Denver, CO. Today, it's the largest privately-owned chain of yoga studios in America, with 160 locations throughout the country. It combines power yoga, Bikram yoga, Vinyasa yoga, and Ashtanga yoga.

12. Chocolove was started by Timothy Moley in Boulder, Colorado. It was one of the first high-end chocolate bars to be made in America. Moley opened the company after he visited Indonesia and fell in love with cacao. The company is known for its high-quality chocolate, love poems tucked into the wrappers, and unique combinations of ingredients, such as chiles and cherries. While the chocolate was originally outsourced for production, it has been produced at the Chocolove factory in Boulder since 2003. Moley has eaten two chocolate bars every day since starting his company.

13. Jack A. Weil changed men's fashion in 1946 when he added a snap to men's Western shirts. Rockmount Ranch Wear's shirts have been worn by Elvis Presley, Paul McCartney, as well as on the big screen by Heath Ledger in *Brokeback Mountain* and Clark Gable in *The Misfits*.

14. Lärabar was founded by Denver native Lara Merriken. Merriken's goal had been to make a great-tasting healthy product. She got the idea for Lärabar when she was hiking the Colorado Rocky Mountains and came up with the idea of a bar that was made only out of nuts, fruits, and spices. The first bars to hit the market were Cherry Pie, Banana Bread, Chocolate Coconut Chew, Apple Pie, and Cashew Cookie. In 2008, General Mills acquired the brand.

15. The Fool's Gold Loaf sandwich was invented in Denver in the 1970s. The sandwich is made when you bathe a loaf of sour bread with margarine and then basically make a peanut butter and jelly sandwich out of grape jelly and creamy peanut butter. Then you stuff it with a surprising ingredient: a pound of bacon. It was created at the Colorado Mine Company in Glendale, CO. The sandwich was invented for Elvis Presley, who allegedly liked it so much that he once flew 22 of his friends out just to get it! He also had the sandwich flown out to him.

16. Justin's Nut Butters is known for being one of the "cleanest" food companies. Their nut butters are known to make great homemade peanut butter cups. The company is based out of Boulder, Colorado.

17. Luggage company Samsonite was founded in Denver in 1910 by Jesse Shwayder, a Blackhawk, CO native. Shwayder was religious and named his first suitcases Samson after the Biblical figure. When the Samson became his best-selling case during the 1960s, Shwayder changed the name. The company has since switched hands, but it remains a popular player in the luggage company. The luggage company even made an appearance in *Dumb & Dumber*.

18. There are many brewing companies in Denver, but Great Divide has been voted 7th best on the planet by *Beer Advocate*. The brewery is most famous for its Oak-Aged Yeti.

19. Sign language-translating gloves were invented by Ryan Patterson, who was attending Grand Junction High School at the time. The gloves translate sign language into words to help improve communication for the hearing impaired and those who do not know sign language.

20. The Slopper burger was invented at a tavern in Pueblo, Colorado. It's an open-faced burger on a

bun, then covered with green chile, onions, and occasionally French fries. Gray's Coors Tavern is most famous for the burger today.

Test Yourself – Questions

1. The cheeseburger was invented by a restaurant owner in which of the following cities?

    a. Boulder
    b. Colorado Springs
    c. Denver

2. The root beer float was originally called:

    a. The Black Cow
    b. The Black Crow
    c. The Buttery Beer

3. Which fast food chain was started in Denver by a University of Colorado Boulder graduate?

    a. Quiznos
    b. Smashburger
    c. Chipotle

4. Chocolove was invented after the founder visited ___ and fell in love with cacao.

    a. India
    b. Indonesia
    c. Malaysia

5. The Fool's Gold Loaf was which musician's favorite sandwich?

    a. John Denver
    b. Elvis Presley
    c. Miley Cyrus

Answers

1. c.

2. a.

3. c.

4. b.

5. b.

CHAPTER FOUR

COLORADO'S ATTRACTIONS

If you're planning a visit to Colorado, you might be wondering about the state's most famous attractions. How much do you know about the attractions the Centennial State has to offer? The state is home to a number of unique natural phenomena. There are four national parks located in Colorado: Rocky Mountain National Park, Mesa Verde National Park, Great Sand Dunes National Park, and Black Canyon of the Gunnison National Park. How much do you really know about these national parks and the features they have to offer? Do you know which road the state is most famous for? Read on to learn the answers to these questions and more facts about Colorado's unique attractions.

The Denver Zoo Started with Just One Bear

The Denver Zoo is the most popular attraction in the Denver metropolitan area, drawing in an average of

1.6 million visitors each year. But do you know how the zoo got its start?

Founded in 1896, the zoo started when an orphaned American black bear was donated to it. The zoo then built Bear Mountain, making it the first zoo in the U.S. to use naturalistic zoo enclosures instead of barred cages.

The zoo later went on to open the Primate Panorama, which had open areas for apes and monkeys and large mesh tents. It also opened Predator Ridge, which features three separate areas that animals are rotated in, allowing them to smell one another. In 2012, the Denver Zoo opened a similar exhibit called Elephant Passage, which has five areas that species are rotated through.

The Denver Zoo may have started out with just one black bear, but today, it is home to 4,125 animals, which are made up by 613 species. Some of the animals that you can expect to find at the Denver Zoo today include monkeys, gorillas, giraffes, camels, lions, spotted hyenas, African wild dogs, snow leopards, red pandas, tigers, cheetahs, and more.

One of the zoo's most popular features is its Toyota Elephant, which was the largest bull elephant habitat in the world when it was first constructed. The elephant habitat is designed to hold a total of 12 elephants, including eight bulls.

In 2012, the Denver Zoo was named the "Greenest Zoo in the Country" by the World Renewable Energy Forum.

This Famous Merry-Go-Round Can Be Found in Colorado

Did you know that Colorado is home to one of the most famous merry-go-rounds? The Kit Carson County Carousel, which is located in Burlington, CO, is one of the oldest wooden merry-go-rounds in the entire United States.

Built in 1905, the Kit Carson County Carousel also the only antique carousel in America to have its original paint on the animals, as well as the scenery panels.

Also known as the Elitch Gardens Carousel, the merry-go-round was constructed by the Philadelphia Toboggan Company in 1905. It was built specifically for Elitch Gardens, located in Kit Carson County.

During the Great Depression, the carousel spent six years in storage. It was reintroduced to Elitch Gardens in 1937.

The carousel is the only surviving menagerie—or carousel that features animals aside from horses—to ever be made by the Philadelphia Toboggan Company. In addition to 25 standing horses and four chariots, the carousel also features a dog, a hippocampus, a lion, a tiger, three zebras, three goats, three giraffes, three deer, and three camels.

The Kit Carson County Carousel & Museum is open to the public. You can ride this famous carousel.

Colorado is Home to America's Largest Sand Dune

When you think of Colorado, you probably think of its beautiful mountains and hot springs. But did you know that the state is home to sand dunes, too? In fact, it might surprise you to learn that the tallest sand dune in the United States can be found in the state! The country's tallest sand dune is located at Great Sand Dunes National Park & Monument in southern Colorado.

Spanning across 107,000 acres, the park is home to Star Dune, a 750-foot tall sand dune, the tallest in North America. It's also one of the most fragile and complex dune systems in the entire world. The sand dunes are constantly shifting, thanks to winds that reach up to 40 mph in the area.

Great Sand Dunes National Park is also unique because there are no snakes or scorpions in the dunes. Additionally, there are at least six endemic insect species, which cannot be found anywhere else on the planet.

Great Sand Dunes National Park was established in

2004. Today, it sees an average of 486,000 visitors each year.

There are several funs ways to get a fun, unique experience of the sand dunes the park has to offer. In certain areas of the park, you can ride horses, llamas, mules, and burros. You can even sandboard or sand sled on the dunes! Be careful when visiting the park, however. During the summer months, the sand is known to reach temperatures up to 150 degrees Fahrenheit, which is hot enough to burn your feet.

Garden of the Gods is Home to This Hidden Gem

Garden of the Gods is a public park that's located in Colorado Springs, CO. It features unique geological formations, including jagged stone towers and fins that jut up 300 feet from the earth.

The giant boulders, rock piles, and mountains in view offer spectacular sights. The park features 15 miles of trails, allowing visitors to get a closer look at the dramatic rock formations.

The Garden of the Gods is also home to a hidden gem: Spaulding's Cavern. The cavern was discovered by Jacob Spaulding in 1848. Located on North Gateway Rock near the Kissing Camels, the cavern was closed, reopened, and then later closed again. It was sealed because it's considered too dangerous for visitors due to erosion and fragile rock. Unfortunately, the cavern is still sealed off today, but one can hope that it will reopen eventually, right?

This National Park is Colorado's Top Attraction

Rocky Mountain National Park is Colorado's No. 1 tourist attraction. The park sees more than 3 million visitors every year, on average. And it's no wonder why. Rocky Mountain National Park is considered to be one of the best spots to witness wildlife in the entire country.

Established in 1915, the park is made up of nearly 250,000 acres of designated wilderness. There are also more than 60 species of mammals that call the park home. During the summer months, 3,000 elk can be found throughout the park. Some of the other animals that you're most likely to see there include moose, bears, Bighorn Sheep, otters, Mule deer, and mountain lions—just to name a few. The park is also home to over 280 species of birds, 11 species of fish, six types of amphibians, and one reptile (the garter snake).

In addition to being a top place to observe wildlife, Rocky Mountain National Park is also one of the highest national parks in the entire country. The park's elevations range from 7,860 feet to 14,259 feet.

Longs Peak is, by far, the park's most popular

feature. The mountain is one of the state's fourteeners, with an elevation of 14,259 feet—and Rocky Mountain National Park's only fourteener. Thousands of people attempt to climb Longs Speak every year.

Rocky Mountain National Park also contains 156 lakes. One of the most popular lakes in the park is Bear Lake, which is located between Hallett Peak and the Continental Divide. It's one of the park's tourist hotspots.

Hikers will be pleased to find 355 miles of hiking trails at the park. There are also 260 miles of trails for horseback riding.

During your journey, you may encounter 900 different types of plants at Rocky Mountain National Park.

The park is, by far, every outdoorsy person and adventure seeker's dream come true.

Rocky Mountain is Home to This Famous Road

Did you know that Rocky Mountain National Park is home to one of the most famous roads in the entire world?

Trail Ridge Road, which also known as U.S. 34, has been called a "scenic wonder of the world." Finished in 1932, it's the highest continuous paved highway in the United States, with an altitude of more than

12,100 feet and 11 miles above tree-line. The road spans across 48 miles, from Estes Park to Grand Lake.

Trail Ridge Road is a huge tourist attraction. This mostly due to the gorgeous views, which you can see right from your car. To the north, you'll see Wyoming and to the east, you'll see the Great Plains. The Rockies can also be seen to the south and west. The road also crosses the Continental Divide at Milner Pass at an elevation of 10,120 feet.

There are also a number of animals that you're likely to see in the area, including elk, bighorn sheep, and marmots.

The road closes in the winter time and is typically open between Memorial Day in May and Columbus Day in October.

The road, which follows a path that the Ute and other Native American tribes used for years, is known to be extremely windy. Temperatures are generally 20 to 30 degrees colder than Estes Park or Grand Lake.

Denver is Home to One of the Nation's Largest Botanical Gardens

Did you know that Denver is home to one of the largest botanical gardens in the entire United States?

Spanning across 23 acres next to Cheesman Park, Denver Botanic Gardens is one the largest botanical gardens in the United States.

There are three locations that make up the Denver Botanic Gardens. The primary location, which is the formal garden, is located on York Street. There's also Denver Botanic Gardens at Chatfield, which features a historic farm and homestead and a natural meadow. There's also an alpine wildflower garden near Mount Evans at the Mt. Goliath location.

Overall, the Denver Botanic Gardens is home to 43 individual gardens, featuring the largest collection of plants in North America. Although the gardens feature many native plants, there are also exhibits of plants from all around the world.

In 1986, Denver Botanic Gardens debuted the first Xeriscape Demonstration Garden in the world! It's still one of the botanical garden's most popular features, along with its Japanese Garden, which is called Shofu-en (the Garden of Wind and Pines). Shofu-en was designed by Koichi Kawana.

Colorado is Home to the Only Cultural National Park in America

Did you know that Mesa Verde National Park is the *only* cultural park in the U.S. National Park System? It's the only national park in the country that's based on preserving the culture of indigenous people.

The park is home to a number of ruins of villages that were built by the Ancient Pueblo peoples, who lived in the dwellings from approximately 600 to 1300 AD.

The area was likely abandoned by the Ancient Pueblo peoples due to crop failures, though no one knows for sure.

Mesa Verde National Park was established by President Theodore Roosevelt to preserve the cliff dwellings. There are more than 400 archaeological sites and more than 600 cliff dwellings of the Pueblo people at the park.

The Cliff Palace is the most iconic dwelling at Mesa Verde. Constructed from sandstone, wooden beams, and mortar, the Cliff Palace dates back over 700 years.

Mesa Verde means "green table" in Spanish. Sorry to disappoint, but there is no green table in the park. The park's name actually originated from the juniper trees and other foliage in the area.

Mesa Verde National Park is home to a pit called "Mummy Lake." Named by cowboys who used it as a watering pit for their horses during the 19th century, Mummy Lake was once believed to be an ancient reservoir. Researchers now believe that it was used for ceremonies, however.

Dinosaur National Monument is Home to 1,500 Fossils

If you want to see some dinosaur fossils, there's no better place to do it than the Centennial State. Colorado is home to a number of dinosaur-oriented attractions, with one of the top attractions being Dinosaur National Monument.

It's worth noting that the majority of the monument is located in Moffat County, Colorado, though some of it is also located in Utah. It's located near Dinosaur, Colorado—yup, it's a real town! The town was actually named after Dinosaur National Monument.

The Quarry Exhibit Hall is home to 1,500 fossils. Located on the cliff face inside the quarry, there are also petroglyphs of Colorado's lost cultures and homesteads that were abandoned by early settlers.

Some of the dinosaur fossils you'll find at Dinosaur National Monument include those of an Allosaurus, Abydosaurus, and Deinonychus. There are also a number of long-neck/long-tail sauropods. You can even touch fossils that date back 149 million years!

Colorado is Home to a Mountain Zoo

There's no doubt that the Denver Zoo is, by far, Colorado's most famous zoo. However, the state is also home to one of the most unique zoos that can be found in the United States! Located in Colorado Springs, the Cheyenne Mountain Zoo is known as "America's Mountain Zoo."

The nickname is fitting for the zoo, which is located 6,800-feet above sea level. In fact, the Cheyenne Mountain Zoo is the highest zoo in the entire United

States. The zoo offers a breathtaking view of the city and animals. The zoo is home to 750 animals from 150 different species. Some of the animals you can expect to find include lions, zebras, elephants, kangaroos, bears, tigers, snow leopards, monkeys, and more.

Perhaps one of the best parts about the zoo is how you can view it. There's an open chair-lift that takes visitors right over the zoo, allowing you to get a unique view of the animals. You can also experience animal encounters, feed the giraffes, and walk through the zoo aviary.

In 2018, *USA Today* named the Cheyenne Mountain Zoo as North America's 4th best zoo.

Colorado is Famous for This Mountain

Pikes Peak is one of Colorado's 53 "fourteeners" (or mountains with an elevation of more than 14,000 feet above sea level). The snow-capped peak is one of the most iconic views of Colorado, often being featured on postcards and other photos of the state. It's what you likely think of when you picture the Coloradan scenery.

With an elevation of 14,115 feet above sea level, Pikes Peak is the highest summit of the southern Front Range of the Rocky Mountains. With its location in Pike National Forest, the summit is higher than any other point in America located to its east.

It might surprise you to learn that even in spite of its high elevation, Pikes Peak is actually *not* the highest mountain in Colorado. In fact, it only ranks at No. 31. The highest mountain in the state is Mt. Elbert, which has an elevation of 14,433 feet.

There are several ways you can check out the scenery of Pikes Peak. These include Camera Point, Glen Cove, Crystal Creek Reservoir, Bottomless Pit, and Devil's Playground. Some of the animals that you're most likely to see in the area include Mule deer, marmots, and Bighorn Sheep.

Pikes Peak is a popular hiking spot. The hike is known to be fairly challenging. The Barr Trail takes most people approximately 8 to 12 hours to complete. Many hikers choose to camp at Barr Camp to give themselves a place to rest.

It might surprise you to learn that Pikes Peak is one of the most visited mountains in the entire world! In fact, the only mountain that sees more visitors is Mt. Fuji. In 2018, Pikes Peak saw about 530,000 visitors.

It's also the No. 1 Colorado Springs attraction during key visitor time, which is between the months of May and July. The temperatures of the mountain tend to be cooler, so it's ideal to wear layers when visiting.

Many people enjoy visiting Colorado Springs during New Year's and watching the fireworks show that takes place every year at Pikes Peak.

Due to the high elevation of Pikes Peak (as well as Colorado's other fourteeners), it's important to take special preparation when driving to the top of the mountain. You'll need to make sure your vehicle is able to handle multiple gear shifts. Also, be sure to let the engine idle once you arrive at the top of the summit.

Colorado is Home to This Famous Railway

Did you know that the highest railway in North America is located in Colorado? The Pikes Peak Cog Railway offers a scenic 8.9-mile trip, in which you will get a great view of the mountain.

Founded in 1889 by the Simmons Beautyrest Mattress Company, the first train reached the summit in 1891.

The railway was operating year-round, but it has been closed since 2019 due to repairs. It's expected to reopen in 2021.

Denver Art Museum Was the First Art Museum This Type of Artwork

Today, the Denver Art Museum is known for its extensive collection of Native American artwork. But did you know that in 1925 it became the first art museum to *ever* start a Native American art collection?

Today, the Native Arts collection is home to more than 20,000 pieces and features pieces from almost every North American tribe, including the ancient Pueblo peoples. The Native Arts collection also includes indigenous African and Oceania art pieces.

Although most famous for its Native Arts collection, the Denver Art Museum is also home to 70,000 other works from many time periods and cultures. Its Modern and Contemporary Art collection includes pieces from Georgia O'Keefe, Pablo Picasso, and Henri Matisse.

Colorado is Home to These Famous Waterfalls

Located in Colorado Springs, the Broadmoor Seven Falls is made up of seven beautiful waterfalls. The Seven Falls are owned by the Broadmoor resort in 2015. Prior to that, the Seven Falls had been family-owned and operated since the early 1880s.

The Seven Falls are:

1. Bridal Veil
2. Feather
3. Hill
4. Hull
5. Ramona
6. Shorty
7. Weimer

Combined, the falls drop a total of 181 feet.

The Largest Hot Springs Pool is Located in Colorado

If you've ever wanted to relax in a hot springs pool, there's no better place to do it than in the Centennial State. In fact, did you know that Glenwood Hot Springs, a luxury resort in Glenwood Springs, CO, is home to the largest hot springs pool in the entire world?

The pool at Glenwood Hot Springs is longer than two city blocks and is fed from the Yampah spring, which produces more than 3 million gallons of water a day. The water is produced at 122 degrees Fahrenheit, which makes it one of the hottest natural springs on the planet, too. The hot springs pools in Glenwood are kept at mild temperatures to 104 degrees Fahrenheit (or the temperature of a hot tub).

There are 15 minerals found in the Yampah hot spring. These minerals are known for the health benefits they offer. In fact, the Ute Indian tribe gave the springs the name "Yampah," which meant "big medicine", due to the therapeutic benefits of the mineral water.

RANDOM FACTS

1. Argo Gold Mine and Mill in Idaho Springs, Colorado offers a tour about the history of the Colorado Gold Rush and the Mill and Argo tunnel. It's here that more than $1 million worth of gold was found, dating back to 1893. If you've ever wanted to get the gold mining experience for yourself, then you've come to the right place, as the mine allows visitors to pan for gold.

2. Broadway shows often take place at the Center for Performing Arts in Denver, CO. Located on the south side of Larimar Square, the Center for Performing Arts is home to the Boettcher Concert Hall, the Ellie Caulkins Opera House, and the Auditorium Theater. Many different types of events and performances take place at the Center for Performing Arts, including those put on by the Denver Center Theater Company, the Denver Center Theatre Academy, and the Denver Center Attractions.

3. Red Rocks Park & Amphitheater is located in Morrison, Colorado, near Denver. *Rolling Stone* magazine has named it the best outdoor venue in the United States—and it's no wonder with its breathtaking beauty. The live music venue and

the city park are named for the red sandstone rock formations that form the walls of the amphitheater. Major live musicians perform at the venue regularly. It's also home to the Colorado Music Hall of Fame, which preserves the history of Colorado's musicians and is home to a lot of John Denver memorabilia.

4. The Pearl Street Mall in Boulder, Colorado is a promenade that acts as the city's center for shopping, dining, and the arts. Located in the heart of Boulder, the mall opened in 1977. Today, there are over 1,000 businesses including many local businesses. It's also a popular spot for street performers to show off their talents.

5. The Denver Museum of Nature and Science is one of the city's most popular cultural attractions. The museum has an *Egyptian Mummies* exhibits, which features two mummies. It's also home to the *Wildlife Halls*, an animal diorama that's one of the largest of its kind in North America. You'll also find dinosaur fills at the *Prehistoric Journey* exhibit and a full-scale replica of NASA's Mars Exploration Rover at the *Space Odyssey* exhibit. You can learn more about the science of taste, Native American cultures, and gems and minerals the museum. There's also an IMAX theater and a Planetarium.

6. Hanging Lake is one of the most popular hiking spots in Colorado. In fact, it sees more than

130,000 visitors every year! Located in Glenwood Canyon near Glenwood Springs, CO, the Hanging Lake Trail is 1.6 miles long. That being said, it's pretty steep and rocky, making it a challenging hiking spot. It ascends approximately 1,000 feet in elevation. Perhaps the most popular feature is Sprouting Rock, which is a much larger waterfall behind the lake, which flows from Dead Horse Canyon.

7. The Buffalo Bill Museum and Grave are located outside of Golden, Colorado. The gravesite and museum honors and preserves the history of the Wild West legend Buffalo Bill Cody. Located at Lookout Mountain Park, the museum and gravesite offers a scenic view of the surrounding area.

8. There are a number of popular Colorado breweries, but New Belgium Brewery in Fort Collins is a popular place to tour a large-scale brewery. The 90-minute tour will help you learn more about the process of making beer and you'll also get to try samples.

9. You can see the beauty of the San Juan National Forest when you take a train ride at the Silverton Narrow Gauge Railroad in Southern Colorado. The coal-fired, steam-powered train is reminiscent of the trains that ran over a century ago.

10. Elitch Gardens Theme and Water Park is an amusement park that's located in Denver, Colorado. The park was one of the first zoos to ever open west of Chicago. It was also Denver's first botanic garden. The park is most famous for its rides The Flying Coaster (a roller coaster on which passengers lie down) and Half Pipe (a snowboard ride). Both of these rides were the first of their kind in America when they opened at the park. In addition to thrill rides, the theme park is home to family-friendly rides and a water park.

11. The Stanley Hotel is one of Colorado's top haunted tourist attractions. You can even stay in Room 217, where Stephen King got his inspiration for *The Shining*. Be sure to make your reservations as far in advance as possible, however, as Room 217 is the most requested room.

12. Comanche National Grassland is a popular spot for hiking, bike riding, camping, and horseback riding. Famous for its dinosaur tracks and ancient rock art, it's a great place to learn more about Colorado's history and see more of the beautiful state.

13. The Paint Mines Interpretive Park, which is located in El Paso County, is named after the colorful clays in the area. Located near Calhan,

the park is set on about 750 acres. The Paint Mines were once used by the Native Americans to make paint. The natives would use the brightly colored bands, which were caused by oxidized iron compounds throughout the layers of clay, to make paint. The Paint Mines show signs of evidence of humans that date back as far as 9,000 years.

14. Canyons of the Ancients National Monument is located in the Four Corners region of Southwestern Colorado. With well-preserved evidence of native cultures dating back 10,000 years, it contains the highest known archaeological site density in America. The landscape is made up of more than 6,000 sites that support evidence of past human life, including villages, dams, reservoirs, cliff dwellings, agricultural fields, and more.

15. Bishop Castle is the largest self-built castle in America. Located in Rye, Colorado, it was constructed by Jim Bishop. Though it originally started out as a one-room stone cottage, it's now believed that it could be the largest one-man architecture in the entire world. Bishop Castle has 16 stories. It's a popular Coloradan roadside attraction.

16. The Maroon Bells are one of Colorado's most picturesque attractions. Often featured on

postcards and other photos of the state, the Maroon Bells are two summits, which are separated by 1/3 of a mile. Located in the Elk Mountains, both of the peaks—Maroon Peak and North Maroon Peak—are "fourteeners" (or over 14,000 feet in elevation).

17. The Wild Animal Sanctuary in Keenesburg, Colorado is the largest animal in the entire world! Set on 720 acres, the animal rescue is home to more than 460 rescues, including African lions, tigers, jaguars, leopards, mountain lions, wolves, bears, coyotes, and more. Many of the rescues were held captive, served as former circus animals, were formerly raised at neglectful zoos or "animal rescues" or were in otherwise tragic situations before finding their forever home at the Wild Animal Sanctuary. There's a 3-mile elevated walkway for visitors to walk and see the animals living cage-free at the rescue.

18. Black Canyon, which is located in Black Canyon National Park, earned its name because parts of the canyon only get sunlight for 33 minutes a day. Located in Gunnison National Park, the Gunnison River drops 34 feet a mile through the Black Canyon. This makes it the 5th steepest mountain descent in all of North America.

19. Downtown Aquarium in Denver is the largest aquarium that can be found between California

and Chicago, IL! The aquarium has a theme that follows the path to the ocean from two "rivers" (the Colorado River and the Kampar River in Indonesia). With approximately 1 million gallons of water tanks, the exhibits include endangered fish, gamefish, northern river otters, Asian arowanas, rainbowfish, Sumatran tigers, and so much more!

20. Colorado is home to a number of the country's top ski resorts. Telluride is considered to be one of the top ski resorts in not only Colorado but also in the United States in general! With 148 trails spread across 2,000 acres, the resort offers everything from kid's nursery slopes to intense off-piste slopes.

Test Yourself – Questions

1. Great Sand Dunes National Park is home to the largest sand dune in the U.S. How tall is it?

   a. 750 feet
   b. 700 feet
   c. 7,000 feet

2. Trail Ridge Road's elevation is over:

   a. 14,000 feet
   b. 20,000 feet
   c. 12,100 feet

3. Which Wild West icon is buried in Colorado?

   a. Jesse James
   b. Buffalo Bill Cody
   c. Billy the Kid

4. The largest hot springs pool in the world is located in:

   a. Colorado Springs
   b. Glenwood Springs
   c. Aspen

5. You can stay in Room No. ___ at the Stanley Hotel, which is where Stephen King got his inspiration for *The Shining*.

   a. 317
   b. 17
   c. 217

Answers

1. a.
2. c.
3. b.
4. b.
5. c.

CHAPTER FIVE

COLORADO'S SPORTS

Coloradans love their sports—and it's no wonder why! The state is home to four professional sports teams. But how much do you know about Colorado sports? Do you know which major sporting event the state once chose not to host? Do you know which famous athletes hail from the state? Do you know how Colorado's high altitude makes playing sports in this state unique? Read on to learn the answers to these questions and other Colorado sports facts!

The First Organized Rodeo in History Was Held in the State

Did you know the first rodeo in the entire world was held in Deer Trail, Colorado on July 4th, 1869?

Okay, so some might argue with this. The location of the world's first rodeo is incredibly controversial. It's important to note that several towns claim to have held the world's first rodeo, including Prescott,

Arizona and Pecos, Texas. In 1888, Prescott, Arizona did hold the first rodeo that charged an admission, which turned the sport into a spectator event. Pecos, Texas claims to have held the first rodeo in the world and is often given that title, but the first rodeo Pecos held was in 1883, which was 14 years *after* Deer Trail, Colorado held its rodeo!

Despite the debate and controversy over where the first rodeo really took place, Deer Trails has been documented as holding the first organized rodeo in which prizes were awarded. The first prize winner took home a new set of clothing.

The world's first rodeo champion was Emilnie Gardenshire, an Englishman. His horse was named Montana Blizzard. Gardenshire won that new set of clothing, as well as the title of the "Champion Bronc Buster of the Plains."

This Training Center is Located in the State

Did you know that Colorado is home to one of the three U.S. Olympics Training Centers in the country?

Located in Colorado Springs, the Olympic Training Center was the first of the three centers to ever be built. It has also been home to the U.S. Olympic Committee since 1978. The other two Olympics Training Centers are located in Chula Vista, California and Lake Placid, New York.

The center is located at the former site of Ent Air Force Base. The location was chosen for its high elevation, which is believed to help enhance training.

The Olympic Training Center in Colorado Springs is home to an Olympic-size swimming pool, gymnasiums, an indoor shooting range, and more.

Some athletes who are training for the Olympics live at the center for months or years, while others visit for training.

Due to the center's location, it may come as no surprise that more Coloradans competed in the 2018 Winter Olympics than any other state in the country!

There was a total of 31 Coloradans who competed in the 2018 Winter Olympics. Some of these included Mikalea Shriffin, Lindsey Vonn, Casey Andringa, Ben Berend, Aaron Blunck, David Chodounsky, Alex Ferreira, Bryan Fletcher, Taylor Fletcher, Arielle Gold, Nathan Weber, Lauren Gibbs, and Noah Hoffman.

Colorado is the Only State to Ever Turn Down Hosting This Major Sporting Event

It may surprise you to learn that, despite being home to the Olympic Training Center, Colorado has actually chosen *not* to host this sporting event!

A number of states have bid to host the Olympics. Some have been successful, while others haven't.

Meanwhile, Colorado is the only state in American history to ever turn down hosting the Olympics.

The 1976 Winter Olympics were originally going to be held in Denver, CO. So, why didn't it work out according to plan?

Colorado state voters were given the final say—and 62% of them voted to not host the event. Their reasons? Cost, pollution, and the population that the Olympics would have brought to Denver!

As a result, Denver withdrew from hosting the Winter Olympics that year. The 1976 Winter Olympics were held in Innsbruck, Austria instead.

Denver's Altitude Has This Interesting Effect on Football and Baseball

You may recall from the first chapter that Denver's altitude helps golf balls travel further. Have you ever wondered what effects playing football or baseball a mile above sea level would have on the games?

Thanks to Denver's high altitude, football kickoffs tend to travel 10% farther than they do in other cities where NFL games are played. In fact, 3 out of 4 of the longest field goals in NFL history have taken place in Denver! Of those field goals is the all-time record, which was a 64-yard kick made by the Denver Broncos' Matt Prater when the team played against the Tennessee Titans back in 2013.

A baseball at 20th and Blake streets is said to travel 9% farther than it does at stadiums that are located at sea level. To put this into perspective, a baseball hit at 400 feet at Yankee Stadium (which is located at sea-level) would travel approximately 440 feet in Denver.

Pitching is also affected by Denver's higher elevation. Curveballs are often said to be less "snappy," while fastballs tend to travel about 6 inches further due to the decrease in resistance.

Who would have thought that the elevation had such a dramatic impact on sports? Pretty neat!

The Denver Broncos Brought Back a Retired Jersey for This Famous NFL Player

You've probably heard that NFL teams retire jersey numbers that have been used by remarkable or outstanding players. But it's not often that retired jerseys make a comeback.

Back in 1963, the Denver Broncos retired jersey No. 18 in honor of Frank Tripucka, who was the team's original quarterback.

Tripucka's jersey number was later un-retired in 2012 when Peyton Manning became a part of the team. It's worth noting, however, that this move was only made with the blessing of Tripucka. Tripucka wanted the former Colts sensation to have his number!

It turned out to be a great decision. Peyton Manning

was the starting quarterback for the Broncos from 2012 to 2015, during which time he helped lead the team to the top of their division. In 2015, Manning ended his NFL career with a Broncos Super Bowl win.

This Late Actor Was the Denver Broncos' First Male Cheerleader

Did you know that the first male "cheerleader" for the Denver Broncos was actually a famous actor? Do you know who?

Robin Williams!

Okay, so Williams wasn't a cheerleader in the way that you're thinking.

In 1979, the actor showed up at one of the Broncos' home games wearing boots and a glittering mini-skirt! Williams waved his pom-poms and rallied 74,000 Broncos fans.

We wish that Williams did this all because he was a huge Broncos fan, but that wasn't the reasoning. He did it all as Mork, his character in the then-popular *Mork & Mindy*!

It wasn't until 14 days later that people learned Williams did it all for the show. Footage from the stunt appeared in an episode from Season 2 of *Mork & Mindy*.

The Broncos Hold One of the Biggest Victory Games in History of the NFL

Did you know that the Broncos hold one of the biggest victory games in the history of the NFL?

It was all thanks to John Elway's come-from-behind victory, which happened at the AFC championship game in 1986-1987. Known as "The Drive," the victory is one of the biggest wins in NFL history!

The Broncos were playing at the Cleveland Browns' stadium. They were thought to be doomed to lose the game because Browns' fans intentionally tried to make them fail by driving around their hotel and honking. This perhaps makes the Broncos' win even more remarkable.

The Denver Broncos Hold the Most Lopsided Super Bowl Score in History

Did you know that, as of 2019, the Denver Broncos hold the record for the most lopsided Super Bowl score in the history of the NFL? This record loss happened in 1990 when the team lost Super Bowl XXIV to the San Francisco 49ers, with a score of 55-10!

It's not the first time the Broncos lost the Super Bowl, either. They lost Super Bowl XXI to the New York Giants (39-20) and Super Bowl XXII to the Washington Redskins (42-10).

The Broncos have also won the Super Bowl on three occasions. The team defeated the Green Bay Packers in 1998 (31-24), the Atlanta Falcons in 1999 (34-19), and the Carolina Panthers in 2016 (24-10).

This NBA Star is From the State

Did you know that former NBA player Chauncey "Mr. Big Shot" Billups is from the Centennial State?

Billups was born in Denver, CO. He attended George Washington High School in Denver where he had a number of basketball successes. Billups was named Colorado Mr. Basketball three times and Colorado Player of the Year twice. He was also a four-time All-State first team pick.

Chauncey Billups later went on to attend the University of Colorado, where he was a basketball star. When he played for the University of Colorado Buffaloes, Billups led the team to the first NCAA tournament in 28 years.

He was chosen third overall by the Boston Celtics in the 1997 NBA draft. Over the course of his career, Billups played for the Celtics, the Toronto Raptors, the Denver Nuggets, the Minnesota Timberwolves, the Detroit Pistons, the New York Knicks, and the Los Angeles Clippers.

Billups earned his nickname after scoring late-game shots with the Detroit Pistons when the beat the Los

Angeles Lakers in the Finals back in 2004. As a result of the game, Billups won the NBA Finals MVP that year.

This Historical Heavyweight Boxing Champion is From Colorado

Did you know that the late heavyweight boxing champion William "Jack" Dempsey was from the Centennial State? Dempsey, who was also known as "Kid Blackie" and "The Manassa Mauler", was the world heavyweight boxing champion between 1919 and 1926.

William Dempsey's life started out in Manassa, Colorado, where he was born into a poor family. The family moved a lot, however, and Dempsey quit elementary school in order to work. He left home when he was 16 years old.

Dempsey didn't have much money and often traveled underneath trains and slept in homeless camps. Since he was desperate for money, he would go to saloons and challenge people to a fight. When his challenges were accepted, people would place bets. Dempsey wrote in his autobiography that he seldom lost these bar fights.

While Dempsey used the pseudonym "Kid Blackie" early in his career, he later went on to fight under the name "Jack Dempsey" after he substituted for his brother who fought under the same name and decided to back out f a fight with George Copelin. Copelin was angry about the replacement in the fight and told the promoter he might kill Dempsey, who weighed 20 pounds less than him. The fight turned out to be a success for Dempsey, who downed Copelin six times in the first round and twice in the second round. The referee stopped the fight after a final knockdown of Copelin in the seventh round. Dempsey did not get paid for the fight, due to the stunt he and his brother had pulled with the switch.

Dempsey went on to become a world heavyweight champion. He was ranked No. 10 on *The Ring* magazine's list of all-time heavyweights. He was also inducted into the International Boxing Hall of Fame.

This Colorado Team Holds a Surprising Record

Did you know that the Colorado Rockies hold the record for the highest MLB season attendance? One might think that the highest all-time attendance record would go to the New York Yankees or the Boston Red Sox, but you'd be wrong!

This attendance record is thanks to the Rockies' first season. During the team's inaugural season in 1993 at Mile High Stadium, there were more than 4.48 million fans in attendance!

Even though the inaugural season was the team's highest season for attendance, the Rockies have still kept a pretty consistent record for attendance. In 2017, the team had the 8th highest attendance record, with more than 2.95 million fans in attendance for the entire season.

The Colorado Avalanche Hold This NHL Record

Did you know that the Colorado Avalanche holds a unique NHL record?

The team was originally founded as the Quebec Nordiques and were a part of the World Hockey Association. When the World Hockey Association and the National Hockey League merged in 1979, the Nordiques joined the NHL. During the 1994-1995 season, the team was sold and relocated to Denver.

During their first season in Denver, the Avalanche won the Pacific Division and then went on to sweep the Florida Panthers in the 1996 Stanley Cup Finals. This made the Avalanche the first and *only* NHL team to ever win the Stanley Cup in the season following a relocation.

In fact, they are one of only two teams of *any* professional sports league to ever hold this record! (The other team is the NFL's Washington Redskins).

In addition, the Avalanche's Stanley Cup win in 1996 was the first sports championship ever won by any Denver-based sports team.

This Former Olympic Gold Medalist Hails from the State

Did you know that former competitive swimmer Amy Van Dyken is from Colorado?

Van Dyken was born in Denver, Colorado. When she was in high school, she placed 4th in the 50-meter freestyle in the 1992 U.S. Olympic Trials. This meant that she just barely missed making the Olympic team.

Amy Van Dyken went to the University of Arizona for college before she transferred to Colorado State University. At the 1994 NCAA championships, Van Dyke was named the Female Swimmer of the Year.

Once Van Dyken finished college, she moved the U.S. Olympic Training Center in Colorado Springs where she trained full-time for the 1996 Olympics.

The rest is history! Throughout her career, Van Dyken went on to win six Olympic gold medals, including four that she won at the 1996 Summer Olympics. She became the first American woman to accomplish this feat and also was the most successful athlete at the 1996 Summer Olympics.

Tragically, Amy Van Dyken's athletic career came to a halt when she was injured in an ATV accident that left her paralyzed from the waist down.

Goose Gossage Hails from Colorado

Did you know that former Major League Baseball player Richard "Goose" Gossage is from Colorado?

Gossage grew up in Colorado Springs, where he attended Wasson High School. He was chosen by the Chicago White Sox in the ninth round of the 1970 MLB draft.

Over the course of his 22-year baseball career, Goose Gossage went on to pitch for nine different teams, with the highlight of his career being spent with the New York Yankees and the San Diego Padres.

Over the course of his career, Gossage set several records. He once ranked at No. 3 for major-league career games pitched. Today, he stills ranks at No. 3 in wins in relief and innings pitched in relief. Gossage also holds the record for blown saves.

Goose Gossage was inducted into the Baseball Hall of Fame in 2008. And to think that it all started out in Colorado Springs!

This Former MLB Player Was Also from Colorado

Did you know that the late MLB player Harry "Doc" Halladay III was born in Denver, Colorado?

Halladay grew up in Arvada. His love for baseball began at a young age. He tried every position on the baseball field. When he was 13 years old, Holladay began to train with Bus Campbell, who had also trained Goose Gossage and Brad Lidge. By the age of 14, his position as a pitcher had already begun to attract major league scouts.

When Halladay graduated from Arvada West High School, he was selected by the Toronto Blue Jays in the first round of the 1995 MLB draft. Harry Halladay played for the Blue Jays from 1998 until 2009 when he was traded to the Philadelphia Phillies, for which he played until 2013.

Over the course of his career, Halladay set a number of records, including becoming the 5th pitcher in MLB history to throw multiple no-hitters during the same season and pitching the 20th perfect game in MLB history.

Harry Halladay was killed in a plane crash in 2017. The Blue Jays retired his jersey number (32) in 2018.

In 2019, Halladay was inducted into the National Baseball Hall of Fame. He was the first player to be elected after death since Roberto Clemente in 1973.

RANDOM FACTS

1. The Denver Broncos currently play their home games at Broncos Stadium at Mile High. Before that, the team played at Mile High Stadium between the years of 1960 and 2000.

2. The Denver Broncos got their name as the result of a contest to name the team in 1960.

3. Denver Broncos fans haven't all been fond of the team's logo, which is a horse head. The logo made its debut in 1997 and, shortly after, someone drove past the team's training facilities and shot paintballs at it.

4. The first NFL African-American placekicker was Gene Mingo, who played for the Broncos between the years of 1960 and 1964.

5. Legendary Broncos quarterback John Elway once played for a New York Yankees farm team during the summer of 1982. He played 42 games and had a .318 batting average.

6. The Colorado Rockies play their home games at Coors Field, which is located in LoDo Denver. They also played at Mile High Stadium from 1993 to 1994.

7. Coors Field is the 3rd oldest National League stadium. It was built in 1995.

8. The Colorado Rockies got their name in 1989 when they became an expansion team. "Rockies" referred to the Rocky Mountains in the area. The name had also previously been used by an NHL team in the Denver area that played from 1976 to 1982.

9. At Coors Field, the purple seats are a mile high. The 20th row seats of the upper deck are 5,280 feet high, which is exactly 80 feet higher than the playing field itself.

10. The Colorado Rockies mascot is a dinosaur. The mascot, which is named Dinger, was chosen due to the dinosaur skull that was found on the stadium grounds when it was first constructed.

11. The Colorado Rockies played against the Boston Red Sox in the World Series in 2007. They were swept by the Red Sox, who defeated them 59-15 over their seven final games. The Rockies were the second team to ever be swept during the World Series. (The first was Oakland Athletic in 1990).

12. Back in 1999, 303 home runs were hit at Coors Field. This is the highest number of home runs that have been hit at any ballpark during one season.

13. Coors Field has heated grass and a heated infield. This is to help melt the snow in early spring and fall. It also helps keep the grass green during the dry Coloradan summers.

14. Coors Field is one of the ballparks with the most cycles hit. The other ballpark is Fenway Park. This is a pretty remarkable feat, considering Fenway Park is much older than Coors Field.

15. Colorado Rockies player Nolan Arenado had one of the most memorable cycles in the history of the MLB hit in a ballpark during the 2017 season.

16. The Colorado Avalanche has won nine division titles. Their first eight division titles were won in Denver and it was the longest streak in the history of the NHL. They qualified for playoffs during their first 10 seasons in Denver. The Avalanche's streak ended in 2007.

17. The Avalanche play their home games at the Pepsi Center in Denver.

18. Several other names were considered for the Colorado Avalanche. The team could have been the Extreme, the Blizzards or the Black Bears. At one point, the "Rocky Mountain Extreme" was chosen, but when *The Denver Post* leaked the name, fans reacted very negatively towards it. The Colorado Extreme was officially chosen instead in 1995.

19. The Denver Nuggets had several names. The NBA team was originally founded as the Denver Lakes back in 1967. Prior to the team's first season, the name was chosen to the Denver Rockets. In 1974, the team was renamed the Nuggets, which it remains today.

20. The Cherry Hills Country Club, which is located in Cherry Hills Village, CO, has hosted professional golf tournaments. Some of these include the U.S. Open and the PGA Championship.

Test Yourself – Questions

1. The first organized rodeo in the world was held in ____.

   a. Aspen, CO
   b. Denver, CO
   c. Deer Trail, CO

2. Which year did Colorado turn down hosting the Winter Olympics?

   a. 1976
   b. 1970
   c. 2006

3. The first Denver-based team to ever a championship was:

   a. The Avalanche
   b. Denver Nuggets
   c. The Broncos

4. The Broncos hold one of the biggest victories in NHL history thanks to…

   a. Peyton Manning
   b. Terrell Davis
   c. John Elway

5. Football kickoffs in Denver travel ___ farther than they do in other cities due to the high altitude.

   a. 1%
   b. 10%
   c. 25%

Answers

1. c.

2. a.

3. a.

4. c.

5. b.

CHAPTER SIX

COLORADO'S URBAN LEGENDS, UNSOLVED MYSTERIES, AND OTHER WEIRD FACTS!

Like other states, Colorado is home to a number of unsolved mysteries, urban legends, haunted spots, and other weird happenings. Do you know of any of the state's biggest unsolved mysteries? Do you know about the most haunted roads in Colorado? There's actually more than one! Do you know which legendary creatures are believed to be found in the state? Have you heard of the area of Colorado that's said to attract UFOs? Do you know about the mysterious deaths of farm animals that took place in the state? Have you heard that there might actually still be prehistoric creatures still roaming the earth in Colorado? To find out the answers to these and other facts about Colorado's most unusual phenomena, read on!

One of America's Most Haunted Roads is in Colorado

Did you know that one of the most haunted roads in the entire country is said to be located in Colorado?

Riverdale Road in Thornton, Colorado is often referred to as the most haunted road in the United States—and for good reason! Located just outside of Denver, the road has an incredibly haunting past.

The road is most famous for being home to the "Gates of Hell." The rusty metal gates on the road once led to a mansion, which was built by David Wolpert during the Gold Rush. Wolpert had a wife and children. They lived happily until he was allegedly possessed by the devil. Wolpert burnt down the mansion and killed his family.

While the mansion is gone, the spot where the house once stood is said to be a hotspot for paranormal activity. People have claimed to hear Wolpert's family screaming and crying at nighttime.

Today, the only things that stand are the old gates and a chicken coop that withstood the fire. It has been said that the chicken coop is where the demons told Wolpert to kill his wife. Some even believe that the chicken coop leads directly to Hell.

The Gates of Hell isn't the only creepy thing about Riverdale Road, either.

The road was supposedly built on Native American burial grounds. It's thought that this may be why a number of tragic accidents have happened on the road. One such accident happened in the 1970s. It's been said that the driver still haunts the road, challenging drivers at night to race him to the death.

There have been reported sightings of headless animals and unexplained chanting. People have also reported seeing the apparitions of hanging slave bodies on the Cottonwood trees that line the road.

Like most haunted roads throughout the country, Riverdale Road has a legend about a Lady in White. The young woman is said to wander the streets at night in hopes of finding someone to offer her a ride. She then disappears before ever getting in the car, leaving drivers confused.

There's also the legend of a young boy who was fatally struck by a car on the way to school. His spirit is said to walk the road at night. The boy's spirit allegedly smears his bloody handprints on street signs in the area.

Riverdale Road is also home to a hill that's known "Jogger's Hill." According to the legend, a jogger died after a hit-and-run accident. The jogger's spirit is now said to terrorize all travelers who stop on the hill, looking for his killer and seeking his revenge.

So, you might want to think twice about taking a ride down Riverdale Road the next time you're in

Thornton, Colorado! And if you *do* somehow find your way on the road, be sure to lock your doors!

Colorado is Home to a Hidden Military Base

This isn't an unsolved mystery, but it *is* something pretty weird. Did you know that Colorado is home to a secret military base?

Located underneath Cheyenne Mountain in Colorado Springs is Cheyenne Mountain Air Force Station. It was once the U.S. Space Command and NORAD, which used to monitor the airspace above the U.S. and Canada. In 2008, it was changed to an air force station. It's also used for flight crew training.

The nuclear bunker is located under 2,000 feet of granite and has 25-ton blast doors that can withstand a 30-megaton nuclear explosion from a mile away. (The most powerful nuclear weapon ever tested in the United States had a potential 15-megaton blast).

Most can agree that it's a bit eerie to know that the Air Force Station is hidden there—even *if* nothing creepy is actually going on!

The Devil's Highway is Said to Run Through Colorado

Chances are, you have probably heard of the famous Route 666. But did you know that it's also earned the nickname of the "Devil's Highway"?

What you might not know about Route 666, which runs through Colorado and three other states, is that it was actually renumbered in 2003. Today, the highway is actually known as Route 491. So, why was it renumbered?

Well, Route 666 is actually thought to be another one of the most haunted roads in America. A number of creepy, unexplained incidents have occurred on the famous highway. For starters, Route 666 had an above average accident rate. Is it possible that these accidents have happened because evil, demon-like forces are at play?

And accidents aren't the only strange thing that happened on Route 666. There were numerous reports of other strange happenings, with perhaps the weirdest being a black sedan that would follow people at a dangerously close distance. It didn't seem to matter how fast the drivers were going. The black sedan followed them no matter what. The even stranger part was that the drivers would often pull over only to find that no one was behind them at all.

So, who was *really* driving that black phantom sedan? Is there any link to the girl in white, a phantom girl who disappears any time she's approached by drivers looking for help?

The phantom sedan and the girl in white aren't the only things that are said to disappear on the highway, either. A number of drivers have gone missing, vanishing completely but leaving behind parts of their car or personal belongings. The few drivers that have disappeared and been found had no recollection of where they might have gone.

Then there are the legends of the mysterious haunted semi truck. The truck is said to be seen driving down the highway at nighttime or in broad daylight. If you get too close to a semi truck, watch out. The truck will allegedly play "chicken" with drivers before swerving and causing them to crash.

There have also been reports of "hell hounds" on the highway. What are hell hounds, you wonder? Well, they're exactly as they sound: hounds from the hell. They are said to be supernatural, monstrous beasts that follow drivers, regardless of speed. The hell hounds, which are believed to travel in packs, are thought to be capable of shredding tires and causing wrecks. Some even say that the hell hounds have jumped into car windows to attack people.

The worst part about all of this? Renumbering the highway hasn't even made a difference. A number of eerie incidents have continued to be reported, even since the change. Could this be because the evil forces don't care about the highway's number?

We're not sure, but next time you're on Route 666—err, *Route 491*—keep your doors locked, windows shut, and avoid any semis or black sedans!

The Skinwalkers of Colorado May Haunt Drivers

The legend of the Skinwalkers is popular in many western U.S. states. Colorado is no different. The legend of Colorado Skinwalkers does slightly vary from the legends of Skinwalkers in other states, however.

This legend of the Skinwalkers goes way, *way* back. The Navajo passed down tales of people who were able to shapeshift into animals. It was believed that these Skinwalkers were actually witches and, in most versions of the tale, it was Native Americans who possessed this ability to shift into animals and use dark magic.

Although Skinwalkers can take the form of any animal, according to local lore, there's a coyote in south/central Colorado that's a coyote with the eyes of a man. The Skinwalker is said to run alongside cars and hit against the hood before it makes the transformation back into a man. Perhaps the most haunting part of the Skinwalker is its yellow canine eyes when it meets the driver's gaze.

There are many people who claim that a Skinwalker seen outside of a car is carrying a warning to not continue down that road. Travelers who ignore a Skinwalker's warning may be faced with an evil shaman who will appear, out of thin air, in the backseat and cause the driver to have an accident, leading to his or her death.

Colorado May Be Home to a Vampire's Grave

This just may be one of the creepiest urban legends about the Centennial State. Did you know that Colorado is said to be home to a vampire grave? Yes, a *real-life* vampire grave.

Located at Lafayette Municipal Cemetery in Lafayette, Co, there's a grave that belongs to a young man named Fodor Glava. Glava, who was 27 when he died in 1918, was from Transylvania.

There have been numerous reports of strange lights, unexplained voices, and other paranormal activity at his gravesite that has led people to believe that Glava was a vampire.

Let's take a closer look at the facts, though. Glava was working as a miner in Colorado at the time of his death. He died during the same time as a major influenza epidemic in the area, which is likely what he died of. Vampires can't die from the flu… can they?

Even in spite of the facts, there are still some locals who are unwilling to accept that Glava could have been human. This might be because a local paranormal investigator named Drea Penndragon allegedly heard Glava ask her if she wanted to see his stake.

Some people have reported getting a strange sensation when they visit Glava's grave. Others have said that they didn't find anything suspicious about the grave.

Colorado May Be Home to Hidden Treasures

It's believed that several treasures may be hidden in Colorado from the 1800s. These hidden treasures are said to have been hidden by a few infamous people!

The infamous town-sheriff Henry Plummer allegedly led a gang, known as the "Road Agent Gang." Made up of robbers and murderers, the gang's mission was to steal miners' gold. Plummer ended up being hanged for being the leader of the gang. Before Plummer died, he never got the chance to let anyone know about where he had hidden his treasure. It was speculated that Plummer buried it in Colorado.

And Plummer's treasure isn't the only treasure that's believed to be hidden in the Centennial State! It's believed that the notorious Butch Cassidy buried the gold he robbed in El Paso County. While no one has found it yet, it's believed that Cassidy's treasure, which is estimated to be worth about $100,000, is buried near Monument, CO.

So, what are your odds of actually *finding* these treasures? It seems likely that someone would have found the treasures already if they are truly out there, but you never know.

The Black Forest is Said to Be Haunted

Did you know that the Black Forest region of Colorado is thought to be haunted? In fact, some even consider it to be one of the most haunted forces in the entire country!

It all dates back to 1990 when Steve Lee and his family moved to a log cabin in the area. They first rented the home for a year before buying it. Once they owned the property, strange things began to happen.

It started out with lights and electronic devices turning on and off at unexplained times. They also heard strange noises. But then things started to get creepier. Lee's children started seeing shadowy figures in the woods. Then there was the strange odor that filled the cabin, burning the family's throats and eyes.

The Lee family assumed that it was pranksters at first, so they installed cameras and motion detectors. The motion detectors would go off even when nothing was happening. The cameras, however, caught some unusual phenomena: unexplained orbs and rays of light, ghostly forms with faces, and other seemingly paranormal activity.

The Lee family contacted the TV show *Sightings* about their situation, which led their case to become of the most famous hauntings in the U.S. The crew of

Sightings caught a lot of strange incidences themselves. One of the producers of the show even allegedly experienced an attempted possession! The medium who worked for the show claimed to detect multiple spirits in the house, including a son of one the family's friends. Although the son had died of an overdose, he told the medium that he had actually been murdered. In addition to spirits, the medium also detected a rift in space/time on the property, where spirits are able to move freely between worlds.

Dinosaurs Might Still Live in Colorado

By now, you already know that Colorado is famous for the dinosaur fossils that were found there. Although this might sound a little bit bizarre, there's a theory that dinosaurs could actually still be residing in Colorado. Yes, real life, breathing, *living* dinosaurs.

You might be wondering how dinosaurs could still be living in Colorado. After all, dinosaurs are extinct. Aren't they?

Well, that's what young Myrtle Snow probably thought when she saw actual *living* dinosaurs in Colorado—and not the animatronic kind. Back in 1935, the then three-year-old saw five baby dinosaurs in Pagosa Springs—or so she says. Snow claimed the dinosaurs attacked a local farmer's sheep, which led him to shoot one of the dinosaurs. Her grandfather took her to see the dead creature the next morning.

She said the gray dinosaur was seven feet tall with a snake-like head, short front legs with claws that looked like chicken feet, large back legs, and a long tail. Snow also said the dinosaur was covered in tiny gray hairs.

We know what you're thinking. Can Myrtle Snow's childhood account of events really be trusted? While it might be easy to think that Snow just had a vivid imagination for a three-year-old, she's not the only one who's reported seeing living dinosaurs in the Centennial State.

Over the years, Pueblo, Colorado residents have reported seeing dinosaurs that resemble Tyrannosaurs-Rex in the countryside. The creature is said to look like a small T-Rex that stands about three feet high and five to seven feet long. The therapod-like creatures are believed to have big hind legs, small front legs, and a long tail. Claims of the Mini T-Rex date back to the 1800s.

These Mini T-Rex creatures are known as "River Dinos" because they're often found near bodies of water.

Over the years, there have been numerous photographs of these so-called Mini T-Rex. Though the photos have been reviewed by cryptozoologists, they are often too blurry to tell, for sure, if it's truly a dinosaur-like creature or not.

However, there is one famous photo that was sent to a cryptozoologist named Chad Arment that is quite believable. The photo features an unidentified man holding a gun in one hand and what appears to be a small dead dinosaur on the other hand. The photo has been the source of a lot of controversies, with some believing that it is proof of living and breathing dinosaurs. There are others who believe that the dinosaur in the black and white photo is merely a realistic-looking toy. Since Arment was unable to figure out who sent the photo to him, it's unlikely that we will ever learn for sure if it's a dinosaur or not.

The belief that dinosaurs are out there is so widespread that Arment even wrote a book on the subject, titled *Cryptozoology and the Investigation of Lesser-Known Mystery Animals.*

With so many reports of alleged sightings, it seems like *something* must be out there. These dinosaurs wouldn't be the first to survive. It's believed that prehistoric fish have survived to this day, often being featured on the show *River Monsters.*

But is it even remotely possible that dinosaurs could still be alive and roaming the state? Some believe that the Colorado weather conditions or high elevation may have somehow made it possible for a small population of dinosaurs to survive to this day.

So, are you at risk of being eaten by T. Rex during your next trip to Colorado? Probably not, but you can never be too careful!

The Mysterious Disappearance of a Mystery Writer

Have you heard of the disappearance of a mystery writer who was working on a novel while he was living in Colorado? No? Well, brace yourself. This is perhaps one of the strangest missing person cases to ever affect the state of Colorado and one of the state's biggest unsolved mysteries to date. It sounds like something you would see on a *Lifetime* movie, but it happened in real life.

It all started on September 7th, 1987 when Tom Young closed up his bookshop on Main Street in the small town of Silver Plume, Colorado. Young and his dog Gus disappeared that day. No one would ever hear from him again.

Here's where things get creepier. Keith Reinhard opened an antique shop in Young's old shop. On August 7th, 1988, Reinhard closed his shop up for the day. And then something rather strange happened: he, too, disappeared.

There were a number of similarities between the disappearances. Both had operated their stores for about a year before they went missing.

Just a coincidence? Well, maybe, but here's where things get even stranger.

Reinhard had been writing a book about Tom Young's disappearance when he went missing. Keith Reinhard had moved to the area in hopes of getting in shape by mountain climbing and had wanted to write a novel. Once he learned about Young's disappearance, he became obsessed with the case and started talking to people in the town to learn all about the disappearance. Reinhard decided to write his book about Young, naming his character Guy Gypsum.

In July of 1988, Tom Young and his dog's remains were discovered in the mountains near Silver Plume. Both of them had been shot in the head. Their remains were found by hunters in the area.

The last time Reinhard was ever seen, he had been walking towards Pendleton Mountain in the late afternoon. It was too late in the day for him to start a challenging 6-hour hike.

The Colorado Alpine Rescue Teams searched the mountain for Keith Reinhard via helicopter, but they didn't turn up anything. It was the first time in 30 years they didn't find a missing person.

His remains still haven't been found to this day.

Some believe that both Tom Young and Keith Reinhard were murdered. It was believed that they might have both discovered something someone didn't want them knowing, considering they both rented the same storefront.

Others believed that Reinhard may have planned his own disappearance. His wife, Carolyn, didn't believe this theory, however.

No matter what happened, it's safe to say this double mystery is pretty creepy. We also wouldn't recommend ever renting out the same storefront as Young and Reinhard, just to be on the safe side.

St. Elmo is Thought to Be Colorado's Most Haunted Ghost Town

St. Elmo is a popular tourist destination, but did you know that the ghost town is also believed to be haunted?

People first settled in the town in 1878. The Stark family arrived in 1881. It is believed that Annabelle Stark, who moved to the town as a young child, might still be there today. Annabelle allegedly left the town for a brief time to marry but eventually returned. It's thought that Annabelle might actually serve as a ghostly protector!

The town in itself is pretty eerie, with haunted-looking remains of buildings, including the general store that was once one of the town's hotspots.

This Park is Said to Be Haunted

Did you know that one of Denver's parks is thought to be haunted? In fact, Cheesman Park is thought to be one of the most haunted spots in all of Denver!

If you've been to Cheesman Park, you might be wondering how this could be possible. On the exterior, it looks like a nice park, but it comes with a surprisingly haunting past.

Why is the park so haunted?

In 1858, Cheesman Park was Denver's first graveyard.

In 1890, it was decided that the bodies buried would be moved to a new location. Although the majority of the marked graves belonged to wealthy deceased people and were able to be moved easily, a lot of the bodies remained unclaimed or belonged to the poor.

A man named E.P. McGovern was given the task of moving the bodies. He was given a per casket price, which led him to hack up the remains and fill children's coffins so he could collect a larger check.

In 1894, construction of the park began. The land was flattened out to make way for Cheesman Park, City Park, and the Denver Botanical Gardens. However, the bodies weren't removed from the park before it opened in 1907.

The remains of what McGovern did were discovered as late as the 1960s. Bones were unearthed as late as 2008 when a new parking area was being built.

Today, there have been numerous reports of strange apparitions near the park. You can also still see where the graves were once in the grass.

The park is so famous for being haunted that it allegedly inspired the movie *Poltergeist!*

The Tommyknockers of Colorado's Mines

Have you ever heard of the "Tommyknockers"? This old mining legend plays a key role in Colorado's history and culture!

The "Tommyknockers" were believed to haunt the caverns during the mining era. They were believed to be found in areas like Leadville and Telluride.

Tommyknockers are thought to be tiny green old, wrinkly men who lived in the mines. They were said to knock the walls of the caverns. While this may seem eerie, hearing knocks from a Tommyknocker was said to be good luck. It was thought that the knocks were there to warn the miner of things like tunnel collapses and other troubles in the mines. If no knocks were present, it was said to be because the Tommyknockers had been disrespected and left, leaving the miners to fend for themselves.

The belief in this local lore was so strong that it's said to be the reason many of Colorado's mines were never sealed off, even long after they were no longer used. The mines were allegedly left open to make their way out and follow the miners onto their next mining adventure.

Did Tommyknockers exist in real life? We'll let you be the judge of this one!

The Mystery of the Dead Farm Animals

Is there anything creepier than dead farm animals? Actually, there is. *Unexplained* dead farm animals that have been brutally mutilated.

A number of farm animals were mysteriously killed throughout the San Luis Valley back in the 1960s. The animals were found skinned alive and, to make things even creepier, their blood had been drained. Although there was no clues or signs of how the animals could have died, some of the animals' features had been carefully removed by what seemed like an expert job.

The strange part was that this wasn't only happening in Colorado. It also happened in Kansas and Minnesota, among other states.

When the FBI finally got involved, there had been over 100 incidents across nine states within about two years. It was determined that the mutilations were the result of natural causes, but many angry farmers disagreed.

There were several theories among the farmers on what might have happened to their farm animals, most of which included cattle and horses.

Witnesses in the area claimed to see UFOs right around the time that the animals were mutilated. That alone might not be so strange if it weren't for the fact that there was a perfect circular outline that was believed to have been burned into nearby ground. One researcher felt so strongly about UFOs being the potential cause of animal mutilations throughout the country that she produced a documentary called *A Strange Harvest*.

So, what was the cause of the dead farm animals? Were UFOs really to blame? If so, it wouldn't have been the first time UFOs have been spotted in Colorado...

UFOs May Be Attracted to One Area of Colorado

There have been a number of reported sightings of Unidentified Flying Objects throughout Colorado. However, there's one area, in particular, that has seen an unusually high number of reported sightings.

The UFO Watchtower in Hooper is said to be a hotspot for unusual activity in Colorado. The watchtower is a couple of stories tall and is often said to be the best spot to see a clear night sky, as it's surrounded by the vacant San Luis Valley. Many people have claimed to see glowing, flashing orbs in the sky from the watchtower.

So, why have there been so many claims of UFOs in this area?

Experts have long debated why UFOs may be drawn to this part of Colorado. Many believe that it's due to the area's geothermal water. Others say that the isolated location and near-empty valley makes people think they're seeing things that aren't actually there.

The only way to find out for sure? Maybe check out the area for yourself! Remember to pack a camera.

Conspiracy Theories Surround the Denver International Airport

When it comes to airports, you wouldn't think they could be the host of conspiracy theories. After all, what unusual events could really be occurring at an airport? However, there are several conspiracy theories surrounding Denver International Airport.

These conspiracy theories date back to the airport's construction. It was widely thought that there was something going on with the airport due to the $4.8 billion it cost to build and 16 months of delays. The airport is also the largest airport in the U.S. and it's unknown why that is. The airport is actually twice the size of the 2nd largest U.S. airport. One construction worker even claimed that there were five multi-level buildings under the airport for unexplained reasons.

Then there are the murals on the walls. Many people find them to be eerie. Some believe that the murals depict an apocalyptic scene where the New World Order is taking over the world as we know it.

The airport's dedication stone features a Masonic symbol, which allegedly gives thanks to the "New World Airport Commission" for funding the project.

This isn't even to mention Blucifer, the Blue Mustang sculpture. The sculpture has glowing red eyes and greets airport visitors. What's more haunting about Blucifer is that it killed its sculptor, Luis Jimenez. A section of the 9,000-pound horse fell on Jimenez, causing him to die of a severed artery.

Is there *really* something going on at the Denver International Airport? The world may never know!

RANDOM FACTS

1. The Slide Rock Bolter is thought to be a huge land whale that lives on mountain slopes. The creature is said to eat both animals and people. The Slide Rock Bolter was first seen by miners and lumberjacks back in the 1800s when they came out of the mountains with stories about the monster. Over the years, the monster has been blamed for tourists who have gone missing in the Coloradan mountains.

2. The "Ghost Bridge" crosses over Kiowa Creek. Formally known as the Third Bridge, it's said to be haunted. Due to a massacre of Native Americans that happened in the area and it's said that the sound of drums beating in the distance can be heard. According to local lore, the longer you stand on the bridge, the louder the sound of the drums gets. There have been reports of the sounds of hooves crossing the Ghost Bridge at night.

3. Brown Palace in Denver is one of the oldest hotels in the area. Some of its most famous guests have included Ronald Reagan, the Beatles, and Taylor Swift. The hotel is said to be one of the city's biggest haunts. Rumors of it being haunted

started in 1911 after a double murder took place at the hotel. Isabel Springer was quarreling with her significant other, who shot her and an innocent bystander. Since then, there have been claims of a ghostly string quartet playing in the hotel's dining room and a phone ringing due to a former resident who's thought to continue to call the front desk long after she died. There have also been reports of an unexplained baby's cries coming from the boiler room.

4. Cripple Creek is thought to be haunted. It's believed that Buffalo Billy's Casino is home to the spirit of a young girl who causes bar glasses to go flying in the air and also draws on the walls. The Colorado Grande Casino, meanwhile, is said to be haunted by Maggie. Maggie is known to play the slot machines after hours and is often recognized by her rosy scent.

5. The Angel of Shavano is one of Colorado's most distinctive features. The snowfield wasn't always there. There are a couple of legends about how it came to be. It has been said that the angel appeared after Shavano, a Ute tribal leader, prayed for his dying friend. A second legend says that the Angel of Shavano says that a Native American princess sacrificed herself for rain during a drought. It's believed that she presents in the form of an angel on the mountain every

year and that her spirit still helps bring water to the area.

6. Penitente Canyon near Del Norte, CO has a haunting past. The canyon was named after the Los Hermanos Penitente (the Repentant Brothers), which is considered to be one of the most mysterious religious groups in the Southwestern U.S. The group allegedly held their secret rituals on the canyon. It has been said that the group's meetings included reenacting Jesus Christ's crucifixion—even going so far as to nail men to a wooden cross and perform flagellations.

7. A teenager named Leroy Drieth was leaving his girlfriend's home in Mead, Colorado back in 1968 when his car hit a tree. The collision killed him instantly. Some believed that Drieth had committed suicide. However, 25 years later, an autopsy revealed that the teen had actually been murdered. Drieth had knife wounds on the back of his neck. While it's not known who murdered Leroy Drieth, some believe that his girlfriend knew who did it.

8. There's said to be a woman in black who has been haunting Central City since the 1800s. Referred to as the "Columbine Lady," the woman is said to visit the grave of John Cameron, who died in the early 1880s. It's believed that the woman was his fiancée and now leaves flowers for him every year on November 1st, which was the day he died. She

also appears on April 5th each year, leading some to speculate that it may have been the date they had planned to wed.

9. The Ridge Home Asylum functioned in Arvada between the years of 1912 and 1991. The asylum once housed more than 1,000 patients, who were said to be treated horrendously. The patients were often drugged and it's been said that some were beaten. Even when the asylum was in use, it was thought to be haunted. Unexplained noises, laughter, apparitions, objects moving entirely on their own, and children running down the asylum's hallways were reported by both patients and staff. After the mental institution was closed in 1991, teenagers in the area broke into the old abandoned building, which still houses all the old furniture, equipment, and toys that were left inside when it closed. Although the building was destroyed in 2004, the Super Target that now sits in its place is still said to be haunted.

10. Back in 1984, a man named Mark Groezinger was found shot dead in his car near Lookout Mountain. No suspects were ever officially named in the murder investigation. However, a number of people believed that Groezinger's widow knew who had killed him.

11. Emma Crawford was a young woman who went to Manitou Springs during the late 1800s. She

was hoping to take advantage of the healing powers of the natural mineral springs because she had tuberculosis. Crawford seemed to recover at first and became engaged to William Hildebrand. Together, they climbed Red Mountain. Crawford wanted to be buried at the summit once she died. Her death came soon after, just days before the wedding was to take place. Hildebrand and a dozen other men took Crawford's casket to the summit. Emma was said to be stubborn, in life and in death. This was demonstrated when a flood happened and caused a landslide, which led to her casket sliding back into town. Over the years, Emma's body parts were discovered, including her skull. Her remains are now located at the Crystal Valley Cemetery. Each year, there's an event held in the town called the Emma Crawford Coffin Races in her honor.

12. Old Colorado City was an early mining town, which had tunnels underneath its streets that connected to the town's bars, brothels, and gambling halls. This allowed people to discreetly take part in these activities. Rumor has it that the town is now full of ghosts, who continue with their secret forms of entertainment.

13. The Henry Treat Rogers Mansion in Cheesman Park, Colorado was known to be haunted. The

house was demolished, however. It's thought that it was demolished due to some of the strange occurrences that went on in the house. The house allegedly inspired Russell Hunter to write *The Changeling*, which is based on his own experience of living in the house in the 1960s.

14. Roger Dean of Littleton, CO was forced at gunpoint to tie up his wife. Dean ended up getting shot and killed after he fled the house for help. Things with this case never added up, however. Before the murder, Roger Dean withdrew $30,000 and put it into a secret account. Some theorized that this was to throw off the cops. There were also unusual sightings of Dean in the hours leading up to his murder. Although it's unknown who shot Roger Dean, it's thought that extortion letters received by his widow years after his murder had been sent by both a man and a woman.

15. The Ute Native American tribe believed that there were Thunderbirds that ruled the skies above the Grand Mesa. According to legend, the birds attacked the Ute's village and carried children to their nest on the edge of the Grand Mesa. So, the strongest Ute warrior disguised himself as a tree and climbed the Mesa to the nest, where he discovered that the children had already been eaten. The angered warrior tossed

the Thunderbird eggs over the edge of the Mesa, causing them to land in the valley below. When the Thunderbirds returned to their nest, they found that it was empty. They soon learned that their offspring had been swallowed by a giant serpent (A.K.A. the Colorado River), they lifted the "serpent" over the Grand Mesa. This created huge scars over the Mesa's top, which had been smooth before then. A storm raged and gouges were filled with the Thunderbirds' tears, which is what formed the Grand Mesa's lakes.

16. According to Ute legend, the tribe put a curse on the Grand Valley. The curse was placed on the valley when the Utes were forced to a federal reservation. There is one way to get around the curse, and it allegedly goes like this: no person who was born in the valley can leave unless they collect sand from the Grand Mesa, the junction of the Colorado or Gunnison Rivers or various other locations in the region. The sand is thought to get rid of the curse's supernatural effects for the Grand Valley native.

17. There have been numerous Bigfoot sightings in Colorado. What better place for Sasquatch to hide than the mountains? There's even a Bigfoot crossing sign on Pike Peaks Highway in Colorado Springs because there were so many reported sightings there in the 1990s. There have

been numerous reports of Bigfoot sightings in Bailey, Colorado. In 2012, there was a famously reported sighting when two women walking in Pike National Forest claimed to see the legendary creature.

18. There have been reports of what are believed to be werewolves, or werewolf-like creatures, in Colorado. Westcliffe, CO is one of the areas where these sightings have been reported. Is it possible that these so-called "werewolves" are actually Skinwalkers, though? The world may never know!

19. Buffalo Bill's Museum is believed to be haunted. The popular tourist attraction has been said to be a hotspot for unusual phenomena, including ghostly cowboy apparitions and dolls "jumping off" the shelves at the gift shop.

20. Hotel Boulderado in Boulder, CO is thought to be haunted. There was an attempted double-suicide, which resulted in only one death, that took place at the hotel back in 1924. There have been numerous reports of paranormal activity at the hotel ever since! People have claimed to see apparitions, hear unusual noises, and witness lights flickering on and off and doors opening and closing for no reason.

Test Yourself – Questions

1. Which of the following is _not_ one of Colorado's most haunted roads?

    a. Riverdale Road
    b. Aspen Road
    c. Route 666

2. Which legendary creature was said to lurk inside the mining caverns?

    a. Skinwalkers
    b. Vampires
    c. Tommyknockers

3. Colorado's most haunted ghost mine is thought to be:

    a. Caribou City
    b. Ashcroft
    c. St. Elmo

4. UFOs are thought to be drawn to Hooper, Colorado, due to:

    a. Geothermal water
    b. An old haunted bridge
    c. Neon lights

5. Which of the following famous people's treasure is _not_ thought to be buried in Colorado:

    a. Butch Cassidy
    b. Blackbeard
    c. Henry Plummer

Answers

1. b.
2. c.
3. c.
4. a.
5. b.

OTHER BOOKS IN THIS SERIES

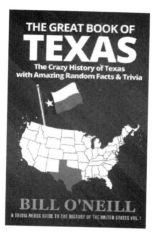

Are you looking to learn more about Texas? Sure, you've heard about the Alamo and JFK's assassination in history class, but there's so much about the Lone Star State that even natives don't know about. In this trivia book, you'll journey through Texas's history, pop culture, sports, folklore, and so much more!

In The Great Book of Texas, some of the things you will learn include:

Which Texas hero isn't even from Texas?

Why is Texas called the Lone Star State?

Which hotel in Austin is one of the most haunted hotels in the United States?

Where was Bonnie and Clyde's hideout located?

Which Tejano musician is buried in Corpus Christi?

What unsolved mysteries happened in the state?

Which Texas-born celebrity was voted "Most Handsome" in high school?

Which popular TV show star just opened a brewery in Austin?

You'll find out the answers to these questions and many other facts. Some of them will be fun, some of them will creepy, and some of them will be sad, but all of them will be fascinating! This book is jampacked with everything you could have ever wondered about Texas.

Whether you consider yourself a Texas pro or you know absolutely nothing about the state, you'll learn something new as you discover more about the state's past, present, and future. Find out about things that weren't mentioned in your history book. In fact, you might even be able to impress your history teacher with your newfound knowledge once you've finished reading! So, what are you waiting for? Dive in now to learn all there is to know about the Lone Star State!

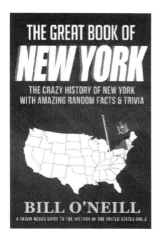

Want to learn more about New York? Sure, you've heard about the Statue of Liberty, but how much do you really know about the Empire State? Do you know why it's even called the Empire State? There's so much about New York that even state natives don't know. In this trivia book, you'll learn more about New York's history, pop culture, folklore, sports, and so much more!

In The Great Book of New York, you'll learn the answers to the following questions:
Why is New York City called the Big Apple?

- What genre of music started out in New York City?
- Which late actress's life is celebrated at a festival held in her hometown every year?
- Which monster might be living in a lake in New York?

- Was there really a Staten Island bogeyman?
- Which movie is loosely based on New York in the 1800s?
- Which cult favorite cake recipe got its start in New York?
- Why do the New York Yankees have pinstripe uniforms?

These are just a few of the many facts you'll find in this book. Some of them will be fun, some of them will be sad, and some of them will be so chilling they'll give you goosebumps, but all of them will be fascinating! This book is full of everything you've ever wondered about New York.

It doesn't matter if you consider yourself a New York state expert or if you know nothing about the Empire State. You're bound to learn something new as you journey through each chapter. You'll be able to impress your friends on your next trivia night!

So, what are you waiting for? Dive in now so you can learn all there is to know about New York!

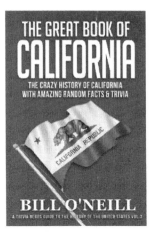

THE GREAT BOOK OF

CALIFORNIA

THE CRAZY HISTORY OF CALIFORNIA
WITH AMAZING RANDOM FACTS & TRIVIA

CALIFORNIA REPUBLIC

BILL O'NEILL

A TRIVIA NERDS GUIDE TO THE HISTORY OF THE UNITED STATES VOL. 3

Are you interested in learning more about California? Sure, you've heard of Hollywood, but how much do you really know about the Golden State? Do you know how it got its nickname or what it was nicknamed first? There's so much to know about California that even people born in the state don't know it all. In this trivia book, you'll learn more about California's history, pop culture, folklore, sports, and so much more!

In The Great Book of California, you'll discover the answers to the following questions

- Why is California called the Golden State?
- What music genres started out in California?
- Which celebrity sex icon's death remains a mystery?
- Which serial killer once murdered in the state?
- Which childhood toy started out in California?

- Which famous fast-food chain opened its first location in the Golden State?
- Which famous athletes are from California?

These are just a few of the many facts you'll find in this book. Some of them will be entertaining, some of them will be tragic, and some of them may haunt you, but all of them will be interesting! This book is full of everything you've ever wondered about California and then some!

Whether you consider yourself a California state expert or you know nothing about the Golden State, you're bound to learn something new in each chapter. You'll be able to impress your college history professor or your friends during your next trivia night!

What are you waiting for? Get started to learn all there is to know about California!

<u>MORE BOOKS BY BILL O'NEILL</u>

I hope you enjoyed this book and learned something new. Please feel free to check out some of my previous books on <u>Amazon.</u>

Made in the USA
Las Vegas, NV
27 May 2023